The White House Story

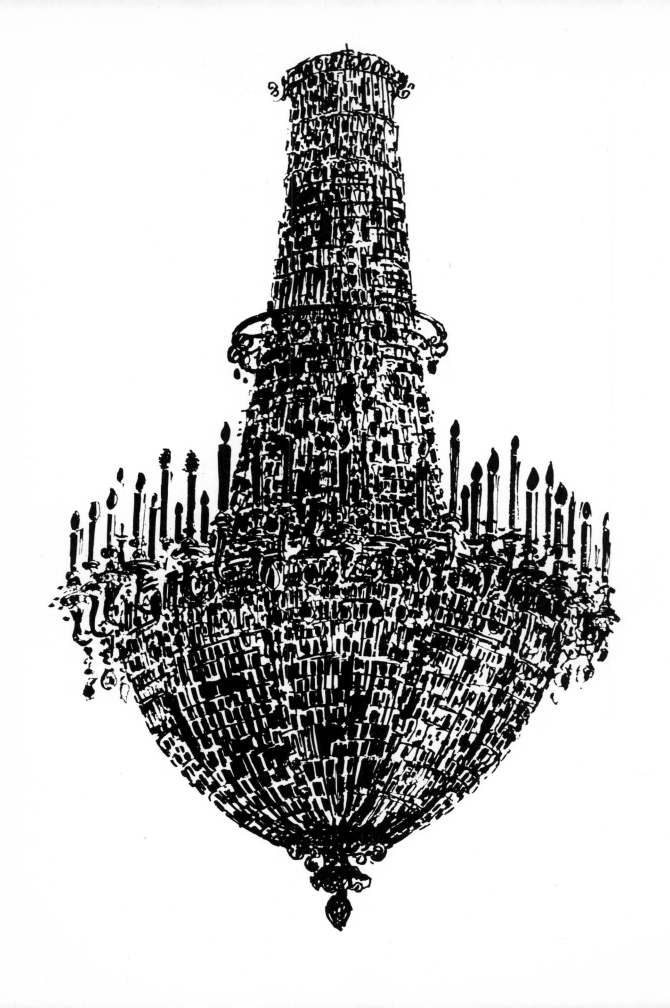

The White House Story

by Charles Hurd

HAWTHORN BOOKS, INC., PUBLISHERS NEW YORK

9389

The White House from the Washington Monument, 1940

Introduction

The White House stands alone among the world's famous institutions. It is, at one and the same time, the name of a building, the nerve center of American government, the example of the nation's constant and ever-growing aspirations, the focal point of the social and political life of the United States, and the expression of a national personality.

From Thomas Jefferson to Lyndon B. Johnson, it has been the background of a leadership of change and growth within the framework of a vast experiment in modern democracy. From Dolley Madison to Jacqueline Kennedy it has supplied an example of the unofficial but absolute leadership that women have exerted on American taste, tradition, and fashion.

These parallel developments, political and social, have made the White House, while always remaining a living institution, the symbol not of a single personality or episode but of an era spanning almost two centuries. And so it still continues.

Enhancing its unique character is the fact that it has not passed into history as a monument to a dead era as have Versailles, the Trianon, the Luxembourg, and the seats of formerly great rulers in Britain, Italy, Germany, and Russia. Never since its opening in 1800 has the White House been more active, more lived in, as the office and residence of the American Chief of State, or more discussed as the residence bearing the personal imprint of the First Family of each succeeding Administration. Yet its symbolism is relatively unchanged.

Like the Declaration of Independence, the Constitution, and the Bill of Rights— all basic in the American story—the White House was conceived and created by the same group of founding fathers. Like the great documents of state, it began as a crude plan, was erected under constant difficulties of compromise, and has since been subjected to constant alteration, enlargement, and modernization. Likewise it has been both the seat and the object of great controversies.

Never formally named the White House until a century after its completion, the building has become so associated with the name that it almost seems to be a living entity. News dispatches relate, with universal reader understanding, that "the White House says," "the White House orders," or occasionally "the White House thinks," as a thin mask covering authoritative but unofficial Executive pronouncements.

In its own history as an exquisitely proportioned stone building, it has been completely reconstructed twice, once because of wartime destruction, and later because of decay. It stands aloof in landscaped grounds behind high fences and guarded gates, but sightseers, sometimes totaling thousands in a week, are welcomed on tours through its public rooms. The White House has never been quite a pri-

7

vate haven for the President and his family, but gradually it has become less of an open public institution.

For more than a century and a quarter, until President Hoover's Administration, when the Presidents were in good health, there were periods when the public could visit the White House unannounced and shake the Presidential hand. More recently the same public, with its unchanging curiosity, has crowded against the fences hoping to see President Johnson strolling at a fast pace around the grounds, often pausing to shake hands through the fence.

The speech of the White House has varied from New England twang to Southern and Midwestern accent and to Texas drawl. But always the words have been the expression of American thought. Once noted only for the occasional personal pronouncements of its occupants, through set statements or more recent press conferences, it now is the background for television broadcasts to the nation and to the world.

In the same rooms provided in the original blueprint, Thomas Jefferson negotiated the Louisiana Purchase, Monroe completed establishment of Liberia as a free country for Negroes in Africa, Lincoln wrote the Emancipation Proclamation, Theodore Roosevelt negotiated the peace treaty ending the Sino-Russian War, Woodrow Wilson drafted his Fourteen Points for peace in World War I, Franklin D. Roosevelt promoted the doctrine of the Four Freedoms and Harry S Truman drafted the speech inaugurating the United Nations. There, too, John F. Kennedy sweated out an anxious night

after warning Soviet Russia that establishment of missile bases in Cuba would provoke nuclear warfare, and Johnson faced crucial issues of foreign policy ranging from South Vietnam to the Dominican Republic.

The main building is a sublime example of Greek Revival architecture, surrounded by elms and sculptured lawns and gardens, with low and unobtrusive wings. For more than a century it housed the President's offices, the Cabinet Room and waiting rooms as well as the second floor bedrooms. Offices have been added in the wings and the living quarters have been enlarged. Later administrations have brought modern personal conveniences ranging from new kitchens to a swimming pool made possible by children's contributions to F. D. Roosevelt, and a bombproof subterranean cavern constructed in World War II as the President's supreme intelligence headquarters, and named with characteristic understatement the "map room."

The only President who did not and could not occupy the White House was George Washington, since the seat of the government was in Philadelphia. However, the East Room, impressive and dignified state reception center, is dominated by Gilbert Stuart's portrait of him. This portrait, painted with oils on canvas, was cut from its frame, rolled into a small package, and removed by Dolley Madison when she fled Washington in 1814, an hour ahead of the British invaders who, with no military reason whatever, burned the building.

In this building, too, Cleveland, a bachelor President, arranged for his own wedding to the young Frances Folsom; children have romped at play, including those of Theodore Roosevelt—who once sneaked their pony up the grand staircase—and the very young offspring of John and Jacqueline Kennedy. Long ago, one President's wife even had a "throne" platform erected in the East Room.

The White House has had its share of scandals: the political plundering and "cornering" of the gold market in Grant's Administration, the dark chapter of Teapot Dome in Harding's.

In the upstairs rooms a disappointed and paralyzed Wilson was cared for by his second wife, who assumed charge of both his personal and political life.

In the cycles of change, four Presidents in one hundred years, from 1865 to 1965, were assassinated, and four men were successively elevated from the innocuous position of Vice President to mastership of the house. Two proceeded to notable careers, two others into testing times for which they were not equipped. The "notables," as of this writing, are Theodore Roosevelt and L. B. Johnson; the mediocrities, Andrew Johnson and Chester A. Arthur. It must be remembered that Harry Truman succeeded Franklin D. Roosevelt as a result of the latter's natural death and therefore is not included in this list.

Many changes in living have taken place over the years. The White House stables that once housed the Presidential carriages and horses—first cleared away with the coming of automobiles—have been recently replaced by a landing pad for helicopters. The once newly created or imported pieces of fine furniture—very few—have become important antiques.

To preserve the individuality and primary functions of the White House without extending its size into that of a small city has required the removal of much that until recently was routine within its walls and grounds.

Until Franklin D. Roosevelt's time, all the activities of the President's office and personal staff were housed within the old building, after several enlargements of an office wing added by Theodore Roosevelt. Today these offices have spread throughout the vast edifice of the State, War, and Navy Building, occupying a block across West Executive Avenue, where it was constructed soon after the Civil War in all the gingerbread grandeur of Victorian architecture.

To the east of the White House stands the Treasury, the only building still serving its original plan among the monumental office buildings (except for the Capitol and the White House) and now more than one hundred years old. When the Civil War started, it was uncompleted, but its thick stone walls were up, and it was temporarily equipped to serve as a last redoubt if the Southern armies should invade the Capital.

Almost the last of the classic customs of the White House to be changed was that of Presidential entertainment of visiting heads of state, who once slept in the mansion's guest room. Now such guests are entertained, with much more comfort and convenience, in two opulent older houses directly across Pennsylvania Avenue from the mansion: Blair House and the neighboring Blair-Lee House. The name of Lee in Blair-Lee House has no 9 connection with Robert E. Lee, but the Lee legend is woven into the history of the other guest house. Blair House was purchased as a private residence by Francis Preston Blair, Andrew Jackson's political crony and adviser. A generation later his son, then serving as Lincoln's Postmaster General, offered, on Lincoln's behalf, command of the Union Army to Robert E. Lee in a last effort at conciliation before the then Colonel Lee resigned his commission and rode off to command the army of Virginia.

In Blair House also, while the White House was being reconstructed, Harry Truman watched from an upper window while an abortive attempt to invade the residence and kill him was frustrated by guards. Two deaths occurred in this gunfight. Through all the years, the White House has survived not only armed attacks on its occupants, but political chicanery and frequent waste and neglect, as well as occasional disrespect and foolish exhibitions. It has not only survived but grown ever more important and dignified. It has become symbolic both of its origins in the roots of American faith and confidence and of the American dream. The growing dignity can be seen from the auction in the Grant Administration of "useless objects," including a pair of Lincoln's pants, in contrast with recent cataloging and permanent preserving of its mementoes.

As an official residence, the White House traditionally reflects the personality, taste, and background of its occupants; as an institution, it is the living monument of the country's past upon which a new future continually is being erected. This is the story of the house and the people who have made it what it is from 1800 to the mid-1960s.

CHARLES HURD

Contents

The story of the White House began on a political theme that is as common today as it was when the Government was established under the Contitution in 1789: almost every major decision throughout American history has begun with a plan or dream; it immediately has been subjected to attacks by interested groups; it has emerged as law through compromise.

The establishment of the Capital of the United States testified to the political acumen of the founding fathers—all mellowed somewhat since the earlier dashing days of the Declaration of Independence in 1776, all sobered by the subsequent debates and compromises that required seven years after victory in the Revolution to hammer the Constitution into workable form.

A surprisingly large majority of the early patriots of 1775–76 were the Government leaders in 1789, although a few notable names were missing. The aging Benjamin Franklin was in his last year of life at Philadelphia. Among the younger group, Patrick Henry of "give-me-liberty-or-give-me-death" fame had bitterly fought adoption of the Constitution and refused George Washington's offer of high position. John Hancock,

Drawing of Georgetown and Washington, 1801

whose bold signature tops those on the Declaration of Independence, stayed in Boston, where he increased his shipping interests and became Governor of Massachusetts, to hold office into his ninth term, when he died.

Among these government founders there was a notable absence of war heroes, with the unmatched exception of George Washington. These political men were the builders rather than the fighters. The most prominent names, then and now, who gathered around Washington at his Inaugural included: Thomas Jefferson, the scholar; James Madison and James Monroe, fellow Virginians and political protégés of Washington and Jefferson; John Adams, scholarly Massachusetts statesman who in his quiet manner had eclipsed his cousin Sam Adams; and Alexander Hamilton, the hard-headed financier patriot of New York. All except Hamilton would live to be Presidents. The question of what kind of President Hamilton would have made was left permanently unanswered when he, not yet fifty years of age, was killed by Aaron Burr in a duel in 1804.

These were the men who led the fights and compromises that eventuated in the selection of what is now Washington, D. C., as the National Capital; who set its political image for the time, and who were responsible for the Executive Mansion that would not be named the White House until many years later.

Three major issues faced the new government on April 30, 1789, when George Washington was inaugurated and there was completed a functioning triumvirate

of Congress, President, and Supreme Court: (1) settlement of the hodge-podge of debts of the States from financing the Revolution; (2) foreign policy in the face of growing conflicts between various European countries, complicated by revolutionary struggles within some countries, notably France; (3) selection of a permanent seat of government.

Foreign policy could wait, and did, but the first and third issues became matters of direct concern immediately after the Congress quickly passed a law that designated Philadelphia as the Capital for ten years from 1790, during which time a permanent site should be selected. The law left only a few months in which to make the decision, but there was understandable impatience because the members of the Continental Congress that ruled from 1776 to 1789 had become tired of moving —sitting at various times in New York, Philadelphia, Baltimore, and Trenton.

During the dickering a large but not very influential group plumped for Philadelphia, which already had played so large a part in the history of the early *pro tem* governments. But there were strong objections. First, Philadelphia was, for its time, a large city, where mobs might easily influence actions of the Government. Second, its selection inevitably would create resentment in other large cities. Third, it had a relatively small but very vocal group of French émigrés —some wealthy—whose endless, and by 1798 tiresome, arguments demanding involvement in French politics would be a perpetual nuisance, if not a danger. It must be remembered that Americans were grateful for French help in the Revolution—while realizing that this help was a move in the perennial war with England —but as free men, English ancestry and relationships became resurgently strong. So Philadelphia quickly was canceled from consideration.

The Capital of the new nation, it was agreed, should be near the geographic center of the country. Because the country was as yet an Atlantic coastal community, "center" meant being relatively equidistant from Boston, the most Northern metropolis, and Charleston, the Southern seaport and regional center.

In a short time the advocates of a Northern atmosphere for the Capital united more or less in backing the town of Germantown, Pennsylvania. The Southerners wanted a site on the Potomac River, near the tobacco and cotton ports of Georgetown, Maryland, and Alexandria, Virginia.

Had George Washington chosen to enter political debates, he probably could have swung the decision to the Potomac without further ado. But (despite Parson Weems's idealism of him later) he did not consider himself as political; he even despised any opposing political parties. He remained aloof. So it was left to Thomas Jefferson, Secretary of State, to argue the case for the South.

For the North, the dominant voice was that of Washington's former military aide-de-camp, the socially glamorous Hamilton, Secretary of the Treasury. Hamilton while still a boy had immigrated from the Barbadoes. He became a leading banker in the States and married into a prominent New York family. Hamilton wanted New York to be chosen but saw it was impossible. He took up the fight for Germantown. There the matter was deadlocked. So the issue turned to the other major argument—money.

Sometime in 1789, Hamilton, perhaps the most astute politician of his generation, had succeeded in getting enough votes to have the Congress choose Germantown as the Capital after 1800. But the Senate did not get around to passage of a bill already approved by the House of Representatives.

In the meantime, debate had shifted to the the debts inherited from the Revolution. These were huge considering the size and relatively small wealth of this agricultural country.

The rich Southerners, particularly the Virginians, with their cavalier tradition about money, had borrowed foreign funds for the war, and had honored these debts and in some cases already repaid them. This was the tradition of Washington, the Lees, the Calverts, and their like.

However, the Northern States had made the logical claim that they should be reimbursed for their debts in behalf of the national cause. Furthermore, some of these States had "discounted" their debts by selling their claims to financial speculators, who formed a powerful lobby in urging the Federal Government to honor this contention. They wanted the Federal Government to assume $20,000-000 of the debt. The South opposed the claims because their population would be taxed equally with the North, which would benefit most from the "stockjobbing." The question deadlocked Congress until a small private dinner party provided the key to compromise. The quoted pas- 15 sages following are Jefferson's own words:

As I was going to the President's one day, I met him [Hamilton] in the street. He walked me backward and forward before the President's door for half an hour. He painted pathetically the temper into which the Legislature had been wrought, and the disgust of those who were called the creditor States, the danger of the secession of their members, and the separation of the States.

He observed that the members of the Administration ought to work in concert; that though the question was not in my Department, yet a common duty should make it a common concern; that the President was the center on which all the administrative questions ultimately rested, and that all of us should rally round him; and that, the question having been lost [in the preceding Congress] by a small majority only, it was probable that an appeal from me to the judgment and discretion of some of my friends might affect a change in the vote, and the machine of government, now suspended, might be set in motion again.

I told him that I was really a stranger to the whole subject; not having informed myself of the system of finance adopted, I knew not how far this was a necessary sequence; that undoubtedly, if its rejection endangered a dissolution of our Union at this incipient stage, I should deem that the most unfortunate of all consequence, to avert which all partial and temporary evils should be yielded. I proposed to him, however, to dine with me the next day, and I would invite another friend or two; bring them into conference together, and I thought it impossible that reasonable men, consulting together coolly, could fail by some mutual sacrifices of opinion, to form a compromise which was to save the Union.

The discussion took place. I could take no part in it but an exhortatory one, because I was a stranger in the circumstances that should govern it. But it was finally agreed that, whatever importance had been attached to the rejection of this proposition, the preservation of the Union and of concord among the States was more important and that therefore it would be better that the vote of rejection should be rescinded, to effect which some members should change their votes. But it was observed

The City of Washington from beyond the Navy Yard, 18—

that this bill would be peculiarly bitter to the Southern States, and that some concomitant measure should be adopted to sweeten it a little to them.

There had been propositions to fix the seat of government either at Philadelphia, at Germantown, or on the Potomac, and it was thought that by giving it to Philadelphia for ten years more, and to Georgetown [Maryland] permanently afterwards, this might, as an anodyne, calm in some degree the ferment which might be excited by the other measure also.

So two of the Potomac members agreed to change their votes and Hamilton undertook to carry the other point. In doing this, the influence he had established over the eastern members, with the agency of Robert Morris with those of the Middle States effected his side of the engagement, and so the assumption was passed, and twenty millions of stock divided among favored States and thrown in as a pabulum to the stock-jobbing herd.

This deal made, George Washington approved it, as he wished to do in any event.

One more compromise remained; the seriousness with which it was argued is difficult to understand in retrospect. Some slight feeling existed that Virginia was too dominant in national affairs and that little Maryland was, if not Northern, at least neutral.

Thus when the site of the new Capital was decreed by law, it was laid out on maps as a rectangular site ten miles square roughly divided in the center by the Potomac River and including areas both in Maryland and Virginia. However, the law provided that no government building was to be erected on the Virginia side. In future years, the Federal Government "ceded" back to Virginia the territory which it could not use. Then, ironically, in the Civil War it confiscated Robert E. Lee's great estate at Arlington and made it the National Cemetery. And in later years much of the former Virginia land became the sites of the National Airport, the Pentagon, and other massive Federal structures.

E Street in Washington, 1817

ORIGINAL DESIGN FOR THE WHITE HOUSE, BY JAMES HOBAN, 1792.

From the collection of Mr. Glenn Brown, F. A. I. A.

The Building of the House

The cornerstone for the President's house was laid on October 12, 1792, the three-hundredth anniversary of the explorer's discovery of the Western Hemisphere. In plans, anticipation, and high hopes, it was a notable occasion. In actual fact it was dreary, frustrating, and almost frightening to realists in the new government. Soon the erection of the establishment would come down to a test of strength between Washington and Jefferson; and the political hostility between Jefferson and Hamiliton would make any financial co-operation from the Secretary of the Treasury impossible. However, the cornerstone did get well and truly laid after long months of surveys and dedicated work by a team of engineers almost providential in their combined skills if extravagant in their plans.

It had been planned that the city, named the Territory of Columbia, would be laid out with broad avenues and many parks. The Capitol would be erected on the only hill in the area, and a mile west would be the mansion, centered in an eighty-acre plot on the bank of the Potomac River. The mansion was to be surrounded in the future by country-like estates, while it was planned that the city's growth would be encouraged to the east. Thus the President would live about midway between Capitol Hill to the east and the busy little port city of Georgetown to the west.

Pierre Charles L'Enfant, son of a French artist with some training in archi-

tecture and engineering, was chosen by Washington to survey the new National Capital. Washington knew well the young Frenchman who had joined the American Revolution in 1777 to serve at his own expense, and who emerged with a major's commission.

The surveyor's plan won Washington's approval, and the new area was quickly termed a City of Magnificent Distances. It was unlike anything in America, and in some degree highly practical in its location of the heaviest construction near water courses, the Potomac and the Tiber Rivers, up which quarried stone could be moved economically on barges. But there were no provisions to develop the swamps, which would not drain themselves, into public water supplies or sewers. The map became a pretty picture, and not a plan, never appreciated until 1901 when the Capital Planning Commission attempted to restore some of its salient features to the city.

Two architects won awards for the design and construction of the White House and the Capitol. James Hoban won the contest for the White House with a design for a building 160 feet long and four stories in height. Dr. William Thornton won the award as architect of the Capitol.

In the new government's first flush of enthusiasm, the financing of the grand scheme seemed deceptively easy. Virginia and Maryland each agreed to make some modest cash advances to help the work get started. Thereafter, the new project

A water color made by architect Benjamin Henry Latrobe showing the porticoes and terraces which he and Jefferson planned to add to the original structure, 1807

would be self-financing through the sale of building lots to the anticipated hordes of well-to-do patriots who would wish to live in the new metropolis and the tradesmen who would establish businesses to serve them. Here was a wonderful idea, if it would work.

However, at the first auction of building lots, held with considerable fanfare and attended personally by Washington, in Gadsby's Tavern, in Alexandria, only thirty lots were sold. This was disheartening, but not enough to discourage the dream, and Hoban and Benjamin Latrobe, who had succeeded Thornton, buckled down to make their plans a reality. As Washington became more determined to make the idea a success, he persuaded Hoban to prune the top story of the house, as a building economy. And the President prevailed on one of his wealthy friends, Colonel John Tayloe, to build, using plans created by Dr. William Thornton—a magnificent octagon house, within walking distance west of the mansion. Where walls curved, the windows and doorframes—even the panes were fitted to the curved form. Washington also moved to pacify a stunned Congress when Hoban was ready to begin the work.

The Irish architect had made his design in return for a prize offered by Congress, to consist either of a cash payment of $500 or a gold medal. Hoban took the medal in lieu of the cash. But when he submitted his cost estimate for the building he had designed it came to 77,900 pounds sterling, or $400,000 in gold money. Here Washington took a hand, writing in 1793 of his work with Hoban:

It was always my idea (and if I am not mistaken Mr. Hoban coincided in the propriety and practicality of it) that the building should be so arranged that only a part of it should be erected for the present; and that upon such a plan as to make the part so erected an entire building and to admit of an addition in the future as circumstances might render proper, without hurting but rather adding to the beauty and magnificence of the whole as an original.

So Hoban dug into the construction job, importing contract-free laborers (mostly German) who erected a settlement in Foggy Bottom and lived there for years while working spasmodically as cash materialized for needed building materials. It was a rule in Government construction in the new city that slaves were not to be used, although it was permitted that subcontractors might use slaves and charge for their time.

It is now time in this narrative to look up and over these rather dismal problems and attempt to glimpse what the Virginians and Marylanders envisaged in their fight for the site of the National Capital.

Within easy riding distance of the new city were families with names already rich in American history, and they lived in houses comparable with the famous country homes of England. Their clothes were made of luxurious cloth and were finely cut; good food and wine were abundant; culture and ideas compared favorably with those of Europe.

The city looked more to the west and south than to Baltimore, only forty miles away, which was separated from it by thick forests bordering Chesapeake Bay. Its most opulent neighboring cities were Georgetown, at its border, and Alexandria, just across the river. Both were important river ports, with close access to the sea, into which the sailing vessels of the day came with cargoes from Europe and the West Indies. In the two ports they picked up tobacco, which held such constant value that a weight of tobacco meant a definite value in money.

Both Georgetown and Alexandria had been chartered as cities since the middle of the eighteenth century and, because the river was wide, each had its own customs house. The countryside around them had been settled for many years. Each plantation was a highly developed settlement in itself with its own subsistence farms, orchards, livestock and smokehouses, farriers and cobblers and dairies. About all that needed to be purchased outside the plantations were sugar, spices, and the luxury clothes and wigs worn by the owners.

All that was really lacking was cash, for this was not a money economy, and that fact had much to do with the slow development of the project and with the failure of most neighboring gentry to make it the location for their town houses.

George Washington—after marriage brought him the fortune of Martha Custis to add to his own, inherited from his brother Lawrence—was considered to be, with his land holdings, one of the richest men in America. Yet his income never exceeded $25,000 a year. Jefferson had an annual income of $5,000.

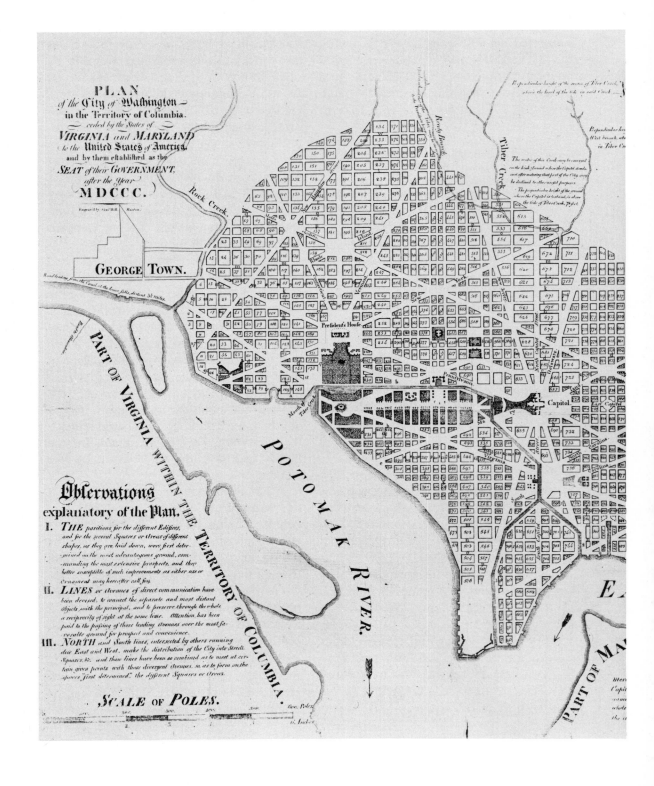

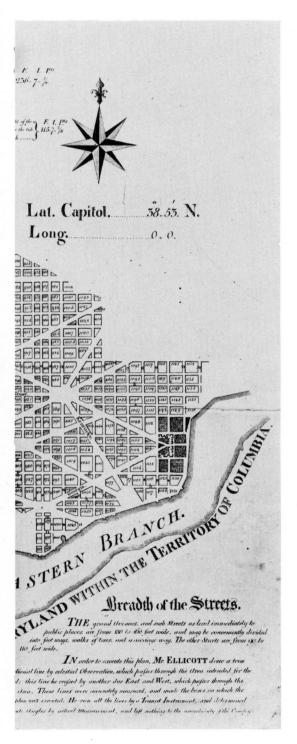

E. I. P^te
256.7.7.

at of the)   E. I. P^te
the tide (115.7.7^te

Lat. Capitol........38.55. N.

Long.........................0. 0.

1 STERN BRANCH.

YLAND WITHIN THE TERRITORY OF COLUMBIA.

Breadth of the Streets.

THE grand avenues, and such Streets as lead immediately to public places, are from 130 to 160 feet wide, and may be conveniently divided into foot ways, walks of trees, and a carriage way. The other Streets are from 90 to 110 feet wide.

IN order to execute this plan, Mr. ELLICOTT drew a true tional line by celestial Observation, which passes through the Area intended for the t; this line he crossed by another due East and West, which passes through the clera. These lines were accurately measured, and made the basis on which the plan was executed. He run all the lines by a Transit Instrument, and determined te angles by actual Measurement, and left nothing to the uncertainty of the Compass.

Plan of the City of Washington, 18—

These were not niggardly sums in the coin of the day, but were picayune compared with the cash resources of the Northern trading and banking families, who from the start simply disdained Washington City—as the District soon began to be called—and neither invested nor moved there except for temporary political chores.

On the Alexandria side of the Potomac lived the more famous families who, as friends and neighbors of President Washington, assumed an air of social paternalism about the new Capital. Lord Fairfax (American, despite his English title) had his seat at Belvoir, on the highway between Alexandria and Mt. Vernon. He had relatives at Ravensworth, south of Alexandria, and still another family of relatives at Mt. Eagle. George Mason was the master of Gunston Hall, and John Park Custis, son of Martha Washington, owned Abingdon.

In this period the Northern cities of Boston, New York, and Philadelphia had their prominent citizens who were building fortunes in the new country; some of them such as the Adamses, the Roosevelts, the Lowells, and the Cabots were already "old families." But, perhaps because of the proximity to the political center of things, the Southerners of the period are more familiar to us than the Yankees. Without knowing much genealogy, those who hear the Maryland names of Carroll and Calvert and Addison usually recognize them as important names from the past.

Some of the Georgetown houses probably served as a challenge to Hoban when he modeled the prospective Presidential house on the grand scale. On the northern bank of the Potomac, in Maryland, was Thomas Addison's manor house named Oxon Hill, in memory of his Oxford Uni-   23

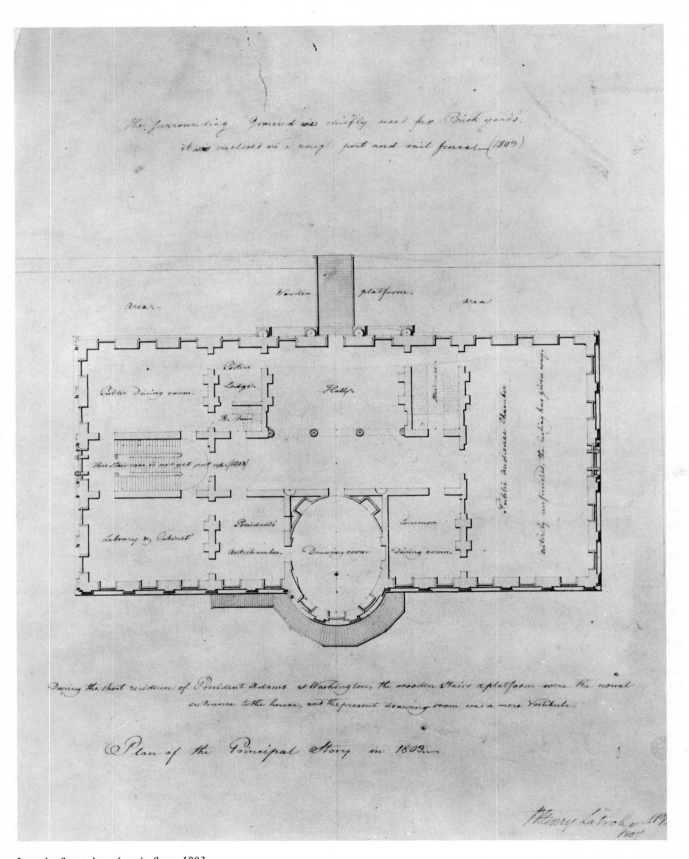

Latrobe floor plan of main floor, 1803

versity days, and just north of Georgetown was the Murdock mansion named Friendship. Many of the older country places have succumbed in recent years to the wreckers employed by real estate developers, but Georgetown has remained almost aggressively proud in maintaining —not as museums, but as lived-in houses —its older mansions that stood there before the map of the Federal territory was even drawn by L'Enfant.

Year by year the two planned, dominant structures in the city-to-be—now called Washington by everyone except the President in whose honor the name was popularly bestowed—rose slowly among the surrounding elms and oaks.

In 1793 Jefferson resigned from Washington's Cabinet in a political breach that affected their friendship only slightly, if at all. Thereafter he divided his time between his own estate Monticello, in Virginia, and Washington.

When Washington retired after his second term in 1797, he returned to Mt. Vernon, and thereafter worked more industriously on behalf of the new city. Thomas Jefferson was then called back to Philadelphia to serve a term as Vice President under John Adams.

This turn-about illustrated the first major change in the new government that would have long repercussions in the history of the White House and lead to future historic contests for the Presidency and establishment of the two-party political system that became one of the great strengths of the United States.

We forget, unless reminded by some special occasion or event, that the new country formed after the Revolution, while a noted experiment in "democracy" in its day, was really a power structure created by the leaders of the Colonies. The Constitution, with the ten amendments named the Bill of Rights, laid the great foundation for the future, but a strong dynasty took the risks to form the United States of America and thereafter ran it as a political holding for many decades.

Even the political enmities such as that between Hamilton and Jefferson never prompted one or the other to arouse mass hysteria or revolution against the other.

It was natural and normal that older customs should continue for a while in the new country. Slavery was recognized as a normal institution in the South, although many Southerners (among them the Lees) employed their Negro hands as free men. In the North, white laborers continued to work in some cases on indenture contracts and most in such poverty that freedom was simply a word to all but the most clever and lucky. The ballot in some States was hedged by many restrictions dealing with property ownership and even religious beliefs until the amendment concerning freedom of religion in the Constitution gradually took hold.

At the time of George Washington's inauguration, it was assumed that President would orderly follow President, without personal contests for votes. Each State would choose Electors according to its population, and these Electors would meet later and choose a President. The runner-up would be Vice President, and in this manner Washington became the first President and John Adams his Vice President. There was only one political party and it was called the Federalist Party.

The White House therefore was de- 25

signed and built as the seat for a President who would represent the dignity of his country, act as a check on legislative action by his veto power over Congressional actions, and direct foreign affairs "with the advice and consent" of the Senate in those matters leading to treaties. His Cabinet was a little group of personal administrative officers, who were to be confirmed by the Senate but thereafter were not accountable to anyone but their chief.

At what must have been some strain on his temper and will, President Washington watched this grand design fall apart while he was still in office.

Jefferson made the first problem when he parted with Presidential policy over the attitude of the Administration toward Europe as the French Revolution—which he heartily espoused by introducing the custom of wearing long trousers instead of breeches—forced decisions as to support or opposition on the Chief Executive. He resigned in 1793, but remained as Secretary of State until the end of that year in response to an almost pleading letter from Washington.

Jefferson fell out for the time being with Vice President John Adams over the latter's extremely conservative Federalist policies in support of the original Washington program. Hamilton made it a three-way contest by adding his opposition to Adams, whom he termed the autocratic "Duke of Braintree" (Adams' Massachusetts estate was named Braintree).

Thus before the White House even had a roof over it, the pattern of future political rivalry was established at the top.

These men were not demagogues, but as veterans of revolution from a day when defeat might have meant their execution and the certain loss of all property, they had firm ideas about the kind of government they wished to form, and each had his own personal following.

As far as is shown by the records, Jefferson was not a notable orator—the pen was his weapon—or very impressive in personal appearance or a good organizer, but he had something out of the ordinary that made him champion of a new democracy despite his ownership of slaves, his enjoyment of almost ostentatious elegance, which in the end bankrupted him, and his lack of political finesse after the government had been formed.

When he publicly declared himself in sympathy with the French Revolution, appeared in public in long trousers, and for a while wore the cockade of the Parisian revolt, he became a "Republican" and soon the country saw the formation of Republican groups that followed him. The groups became a political party, which by some perverse change in politics finally made Jefferson the Father of the modern Democratic Party, as opposed to the Whigs who followed the Federalists and then became the modern Republicans.

All of this political brew was becoming more and more important in the Philadelphia Government and would rise to a climax of Presidential leadership that would erupt before George Washington died at the close of 1799. John Adams first tasted the coming explosion in 1796.

The year 1796 was the first and the last election year in which the Presidency changed hands in the "normal" pattern hopefully set by the founding fathers. Already the incipient White House was feeling the manner in which people and their individualities override institutions.

The Electors duly met after the States had chosen them. They gave the Presidency to John Adams, as had normally been expected, with Vice Presidents following their chiefs into the high office. Thomas Jefferson, who had left the government "forever" in 1793, became Vice President as the runner-up for electoral votes. But his job in itself hardly upset John Adams, since the Vice President was only a stand-by office holder with no responsibilities except to preside over the Senate and in case of a tie cast his vote to break it.

Adams settled down to become a strong President in an anticipated eight years in office, and felt comfortably secure in his Federalist conservatism, especially after publication of President Washington's conservative Farewell Address to the country.

He ruled in Philadelphia as a patriarchal Chief of State until the late winter of 1800 when June was set as the date for removal of the Federal Government to Washington. By the time the move was made, the White House was little more than a crude shelter and its symbolism was being shaken to its political foundations.

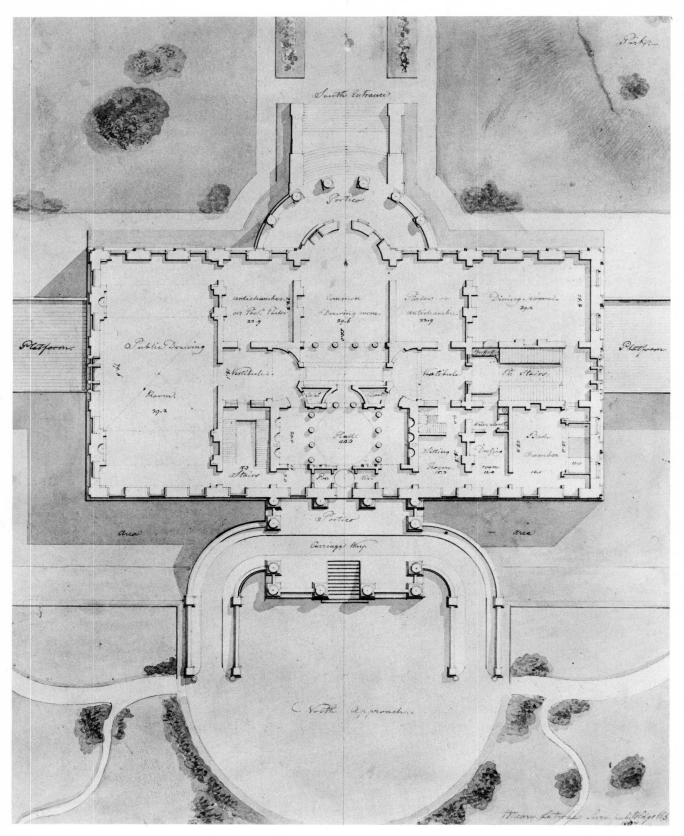

Latrobe floor plan change, 1807

A nation of 5,300,000 people saluted from various distances the "formal" opening of the National Capital, when John Adams arrived by carriage from Philadelphia on June 3, 1800. He was being followed by the 136 members of the Executive staff of the Government, who were traveling, with records and trophies, by the longer and more comfortable water route from Philadelphia.

The event was auspicious in national history, and somewhat notable to the rest of the world. But at the time it was hardly inspiring.

The White House, or palace, was far from finished. The entire city of Washington contained only about forty houses, and the elaborate ones were few and far between. Colonel Tayloe had come from Virginia to visit the Octagon House, but decided against making it his regular residence. Congress would not convene until the next December, so what "life" the city displayed was primarily an echo of Georgetown's.

The President looked over his new "mansion," and shared disapproval of its state with his wife; Abigail. They drove to Mt. Vernon to call on "Lady" Washington, widowed since her husband's death the previous December, spent a few days, but left as hastily as was decently possible for the comfortable environs of their home at Braintree, Massachusetts.

John and Abigail Adams returned to Washington on November 16, thirty-two days after starting their journey from Braintree. They had lost their way on the carriage journey in the forests between Baltimore and Washington, and recovered it only with the aid of a nameless Negro, whose act was gratefully noted in Abigail's diary.

To the Adams couple, long accustomed to the comforts of Philadelphia and veterans of the comfortable living abroad where John Adams had been sent on diplomatic missions, the city probably appeared more depressing than to younger persons with hope in their eyes. Furthermore, while it was not certain, it was probable that Adams would end his distinguished career with defeat, in what had been expected to be an automatic reelection at the time he had succeeded George Washington. So, in a way, he was returning to preside at his own political funeral. In that year, his son John Quincy Adams, thirty-three years old, was rounding out a diplomatic career by serving as Minister to Berlin.

While the President worked and conferred in preparation for the opening of the Congress, Mrs. Adams buckled down to the immediate task of making, insofar as was possible, the shell of a "palace" livable, between paying and receiving calls. Congress had found the sum of $25,000 to appropriate for furnishings of the house, but there was little evidence of money spent. There was not a single bell to ring for a servant.

The grounds were cluttered with workmen's shacks, but it was hard to find anyone to fetch wood for the fireplaces, or to contrive lighting for the long and empty corridors. Abigail's estimate of a need for thirty servants overwhelmed her, and thought of the expense frightened her, but she managed.

Of the present formal Blue Room, Mrs. Adams made a reception room, the Red Room became the library for the President's private use, the Green Room was furnished as a private dining room. The room designed as a State Dining Room served as Cabinet Room and public office for the President. Bedrooms were improvised on the second floor.

The first housekeeping days in the Presidential house were bleak for Abigail, as she revealed in a letter written to her daughter, Abigail Adams Smith:

. . . I arrived here on Sunday last, and without meeting with any accident worth noting, except losing ourselves when we left Baltimore. . . . Fortunately a straggling black came up with us, and we engaged him as a guide to extricate us from our difficulties; but woods are all you see from Baltimore until you reach the City which is only so in name. . . .

In the city there are buildings enough, if they were compact and finished, to accommodate Congress and those attached to it; but as they are, and scattered as they are, I see no great comfort for them. . . . The house is on a grand and superb scale, requiring about thirty servants to attend and keep the apartments in proper order, and perform the ordinary business of the house and stables; an establishment very well proportioned to the President's salary.

The lighting of the apartments from the kitchen to parlors and chambers is a tax indeed and the fires we are obliged to keep to secure us from daily agues is another very cheerful comfort. To assist us in this great castle, and render less assistance necessary, bells are wholly wanting, not one single one being hung through the whole house, and promises are all you can obtain. This is so great an incon-

venience that I know not what to do or how to do.

The ladies from Georgetown and in this city have many of them visited me. Yesterday I returned fifteen visits, but such a place as Georgetown appears! Why, our Milton is beautiful—but no comparisons! If they will put me up some bells, and have wood enough to keep the fires, I deign to be pleased. I could content myself almost anywhere for three months; but surrounded with forests, can you believe that wood is not to be had! . . . We have indeed come into a new country.

You must keep all this to yourself, and when asked how I like it, say that I write you the situation is beautiful, which is true. . . . We have not the least fence, yard or other convenience without; and the great unfinished audience room I make a drying-room of to hang up the clothes in. . . . If the twelve years in which this place has been considered as the future seat of government had been improved as they would have been in New England, very many of the present inconveniences would have been removed.

Abigail actually did not remain for even three months, the time until the next Inaugural in early March when, under the older leisurely custom, the Congress then adjourned until the following December. She held a reception on New Year's Day 1801 and then left for Braintree.

But was Washington so gloomy and bedraggled in the eyes of everyone, as it seemed to the tired and possibly jaded Adams couple?

As always, while the old look back with relish on the past, and find the new trying —particularly when the new is difficult pioneering—there are the young and not-so-young but vigorous who give another outlook. And so it was with the beginnings of the fabulous story of the White House and its new place in the world.

To three other persons who moved to

Washington in the fall of 1800 it was the symbol of the future—the beginning of a new venture in living. All would become part of the new society centering on the White House, would make long-enduring contributions to it, and carve their own impressive niches in its records. They were only slightly acquainted with each other before that year, and they came from widely disparate backgrounds. The three were Thomas Jefferson, Dolley Madison, and Margaret Bayard Smith. Jefferson and Mrs. Madison played star roles in the drama, and Mrs. Smith was the recorder, wife of a newspaper editor, who became one of the first noted American women writers.

The Washington they saw had quite a different setting and atmosphere from the frigid, stuffy, and crude society that bore down on Mrs. Adams. It included the same woods, but these also could be seen as beautiful. It had a scattering of distinguished and charming people. There were good inns at which to sleep and dine, and hospitality was notable although servants were so expensive that Mrs. Smith had to pay her single helper twelve shillings and sixpence a week. There was even a theater, founded August 22, 1800, by a company which called itself the United States Theatre. It gave regular performances, except on very rainy evenings when the streets were all but impassable and hackers charged as much as ten dollars for the evenings.

Margaret Smith viewed the Capital City as a resident, when she rode into it from Philadelphia as the twenty-two-year-old bride of Samuel Harrison Smith, after their marriage on September 29. They were there on Jefferson's personal invitation to Sam Smith. Margaret had never met Jefferson, but she brought from her father's Whig household an admittedly personal dislike for the Republican, even though this feeling ran counter to her husband's.

In the normal order of things, Margaret Smith would have been the retiring wife of a husband who was somewhat of a prodigy. Born in 1772 he had been graduated from the University of Pennsylvania when he was fifteen years of age. By his twenty-fifth birthday he had founded a newspaper in Philadelphia and become Recording Secretary of the Philosophical Society, founded by Benjamin Franklin, and of which Jefferson was President.

Jefferson sponsored a contest for a paper on national education, and Smith won the prize. When the government moved to Washington, Jefferson invited Smith to found a newspaper there and offered him a subsidy in the form of advertising of official Government notices. Smith must have been a persuasive writer of editorials, as his nickname was "Silky-Milky Smith," but he also recognized the practicalities of opportunity.

Smith went to Washington early in September 1800, bought a house and farm half a mile north of the Capitol, arranged to have his printing equipment—also housed in the farm building—shipped to him, married his fiancée, and set off to prepare for the first issue of *The National Intelligencer and Washington Advertiser* on October 31.

He prospered, bought a second home in the "country" north of Georgetown, sold his newspaper in 1810, and became 31 a locally noted financier. Once he was named as Secretary of the Treasury *ad interim*. But that time Margaret was a noted commentator on the Washington scene, becoming principal correspondent for *Godey's Lady's Book;* author of many since-forgotten novels, and the writer of thousands of letters to her sisters, son, and daughters. To her, because of her letters, goes much of the credit for what we know of Washington, the Capitol, and the President's House in the early days.

The Smiths drove into Washington from the Bladensburg road, running close alongside the Tiber River, its valley glowing with the red-budded dogwood trees and many other trees not seen in Philadelphia. There were tall native magnolias and tulip-rose trees with azaleas clustered on the ground beneath their branches. This was truly a Southern city.

Sam pointed out to her Conrad's Tavern, which was the temporary home of twenty officials, among whom as Vice President and ranking guest Jefferson alone had the luxury of a private sitting room.

In the days that followed, Margaret Smith found charming neighbors among already settled residents: Dr. William Thornton, the famous architect, and Mrs. Thornton, awaiting the promised appointment of Dr. Thornton to the post of Superintendent of the Patent Office; Captain Thomas Tingey, former British naval officer and revolutionary patriot, who had been promised direction of the projected Navy Yard; Thomas Law and Mrs. Law, both somewhat eccentric. Mr. Law was brother of the English Lord Ellenborough, and Mrs. Law was granddaughter of Mrs. George Washington.

And there was Mrs. Bell, not otherwise identified, but a fine neighbor. Margaret wrote of her:

I thought I was coming into a land of strangers; but with a husband so beloved, I hesitated not to leave the kindest of fathers and the most indulgent of friends. But here in Mrs. Bell have I met with a mother, for sure no daughter could be treated wtih more affection. . . . Soon the Tingeys and the Thorntons came to pay calls, and they were in her house with Mrs. Bell.
. . . We passed an agreeable afternoon and they were treated with my wedding cake. Mrs. B. brought with her a large basket of sweet potatoes and some fine cabbage.

It would be some time before Margaret would meet Dolley Madison, who entered Washington in a unique position some months later. But she soon met Jefferson, the man who in her mind's eye had been almost repulsive.

The Vice President did not call on her socially. He visited the Smiths on business with a manuscript for the famous "Jefferson's Manual," which he had written for guidance of Congressional debate. Sam was to print it. In the custom of business families, Sam being out, Margaret received the caller, and here is her report, as she later put it down in her diary:

". . . And is this," said I, after my first meeting with Mr. Jefferson, "the violent democrat, the vulgar demagogue, the bold atheist and profligate man I had so often heard denounced by the federalists? Can this man so meek and mild, yet dignified in his manners, with a voice so soft and low, with a countenance so benignant and intelligent, can he be that daring leader of a faction, that disturber of the peace, that enemy of all rank and order?"
In December, 1800, a few days after Congress had for the first time met in our new metropolis, I was one morning sitting alone in the parlor, when the servant opened the door and showed in a gentleman who wished to see my husband. The usual candor and frankness with which I met strangers were somewhat checked by the dignified and reserved air of the present visitor; but the chilled feeling was only momentary, for after taking the chair I offered him in a free and easy manner, and carelessly throwing his arm on the table near which he sat, he turned toward me a counte-

ATLAS

til

Friherre Klinckowströms Bref

om de

FÖRENTE STATERNE.

Presidentens i de Förente Staterna Residence i Washington.

Engraving of White House which appeared on the cover of a nineteenth-century atlas

nance beaming with an expression of benevolence and with a manner and voice almost femininely soft and gentle, entered into conversation on the commonplace topics of the day, from which, before I was conscious of it, he had drawn me into observations of a more personal and interesting nature.

I know not how it was, but there was something in his manner, his countenance and voice that at once unlocked my heart, and in answer to his casual enquiries concerning our situation in our *new home,* as he called it, I found myself frankly telling him what I liked or disliked in our present circumstances and abode. So kind and conciliatory were his look and manners that I forgot he was not a friend of my own, until on the opening of the door, Mr. Smith entered and introduced the stranger to me as *Mr. Jefferson.* . . . I felt my cheeks burn and my heart throb, and not a word more could I speak while he remained. Nay, such was my embarrassment I could scarcely listen to the conversation between him and my husband.

The Jefferson whom Margaret Smith thus recorded apparently masked well his preoccupations as a politician. Perhaps he took this opportunity to have his *Manual* started in publication as something to do in a tense and uncertain period on which the future of the White House might well hinge.

These were, under the Constitution, long days of anxiety in Presidential contests, because the actual votes cast by citizens did not determine the election of a President. They voted only for Electors, who in turn must make the sometimes long journeys to Washington, there to meet and themselves choose the new President. If a majority of them failed to agree, the contest must be sent to the House of Representatives.

It had become obvious that this election would be uncertain and hard-fought right into the House. In the early tradition—which was killed here—Presidential cand-

34

idates did not campaign but remained aloof from politics, but their friends were active. In addition the Federalist Party fell apart when Hamilton, now on the outs with Adams, found it less repulsive to back, of all men, Aaron Burr in New York.

The results were ironic. When the Electors arrived in Washington, 73 voted for both Jefferson and Burr, 65 were for Adams and 63 were for Charles Pinckney. None had a majority, and the issue went to the House, which was just as free to name Pinckney as any other contender.

The House received the contest on February 11 and over a span of days cast thirty ballots before it declared Jefferson the winner, and named Aaron Burr as his Vice President.

By that vote, Northerners were to lose control of the Executive branch for twenty-four years, until Adams' son should recapture it. But in his remaining days in office before March 4, Adams stubbornly proceeded to place in the courts men who would perpetuate by their decisions a conservative tradition—the life-appointed Federal judges. He jammed through a bill to enlarge the Federal bench. And earlier he had appointed John Marshall to be Chief Justice of the United States.

As his defeat for re-election became a probability, Adams arranged to relieve his son as Minister to Berlin, so that John Quincy would not be embarrassed by having this done by Jefferson's new party.

Early on the morning of March 4, before the crowds began to gather to see Jefferson's Inaugural, Adams entered his coach and left Washington, refusing to escort Jefferson to the ceremony.

At Conrad's Inn, Jefferson declined a suggestion that he ride in a coach to the Capitol for his Inaugural. He rode horseback up the hill. Afterwards he rode to the mansion with a small escort while, in Washington and elsewhere in the country, except New England, cannon were fired in salute to him.

The White House received a new tenant, whose election had bitterly divided his country.

Elevation of the South front of the President's house, copied from the drawing as proposed to be altered 1807. Jan. 1817

Gouverneur Morris, third-generation and wealthy New York landholder, brilliant lawyer, a "founding father" and aristocratic snob, traveled to Washington to attend Jefferson's first Inaugural. He summed up his views as follows:

"We only need here houses, cellars, kitchens, scholarly men, amiable women, and a few other such trifles to possess a perfect city. In a word, this is the best city in the world to live in—in the future."

Jefferson set out expeditiously to lay the foundation for this future. From Monticello he took to the White House a staff of his own servants (seeing nothing untoward in the fact that they were slaves). He rapidly made the mansion a livable palace and, being long since widowed, turned to the ranking lady in the Administration to act as an official hostess.

This would normally have been the wife of the Vice President, but Aaron Burr was unmarried. The next wife in line was Dolley Madison, an important accident in White House history, as she was the wife of James Madison, Jefferson's Secretary of State.

From the beginning of Jefferson's Administration, Madison was his right hand and obviously favorite candidate for the succession. Monroe was less in the limelight; already a prominent but relatively unsuccessful member of various foreign missions, he was Governor of Virginia in 1800 and out of the national picture until 1803. So, with Madison as principal aide and adviser, Jefferson set out in his own

way and time to lay many of the traditions of the White House which are still with us in the present.

An ardent democrat and distrusted in the Northern cities as a radical, he saw no harm in slave-owning; he managed his money so poorly that he ruined himself by extravagant living and embellishments of the President's mansion; and, by his actions, he apparently resented any efforts to modify his powers by the Congress.

He was the first President to live outside the shadow of George Washington and did not owe his election, as had John Adams, to him. Despising the Federalists, he never—so far as is recorded—ever talked with Vice President Burr.

Almost by accident, it would seem from the records, Jefferson's genius for directing the new government guided him in appointing Albert Gallatin, the Swiss-born scholar and financier, as Secretary of the Treasury—a post that Gallatin held for fourteen years. Gallatin helped somewhat to salve Jefferson's poor relations with Congress by insisting upon strict accountability of the Treasury to Congress, and by closing his first four years in officer with a surplus in the United States Treasury of $1,000,000.

Gallatin's role in the White House story is a secondary one, but many historians, when they think of him at all, wonder why he has been so neglected. In his shaping of the Federal Government in Washington, and making permanent the dominance of the Presidency in practice rather than on the basis of personal prestige as George Washington had done, Jefferson was aided by the circumstances of his time.

The strength of Congress lay particularly in its power to appropriate funds and in its right to confirm or reject Presidential appointees and to approve or reject treaties. However, Congress was mostly absent. Its members gathered leisurely in the late fall, and it convened formally only between early December and March 4. The Supreme Court held ultimate powers of decision on the Constitutionality of laws, but its work required attendance by the Justices only in the winter months. But the Presidency was a job broken only by short vacations. Thus the President and his Cabinet, which included only the Secretaries of State, War, and Treasury, the Attorney General and the Postmaster General were the Government.

When Jefferson held his first Independence Day reception in the mansion, on July 4, 1801, the guests, including all Government officials and Washington "society," numbered about one hundred. By now the house was well furnished, the Marine Band marched through the rooms playing much as it does today, Jefferson's servants served red and white wines from France, and buffet tables were spread in the State Dining Room. Five Cherokee Indian chiefs, in Washington as guests of the President to celebrate signing of a new treaty, stood rigidly behind Jefferson, wearing their full paint and feather regalia.

This reception lasted for two hours, from noon to 2 P.M., after which fifty of the higher-ranking guests hurried off to change from their hot attire (no concession was yet made to warm weather in clothing) into fresh clothes for a formal dinner served at Conrad's from 4 to 6 P.M. After these fifty had dined, then spent three hours in conversation, the day ended at Conrad's with service of hot tea and a cold supper.

Jefferson's evenings were usually quiet ones spent with favorite company, particularly the Madisons, Gideon Granger, his Postmaster General and a connoisseur of wines, and Dr. William Thornton, to whom he had given his favorite administrative position, Commissioner of Patents.

Nonetheless, if the bachelor-dominated Presidential house reflected the quiet business of its intellectual master, there began to develop color in its surroundings that vied with other American cities, even though everything was on a smaller scale.

It is a notable footnote to American history that at the start of the nineteenth century, the new and small country carved out by Revolution in the Western Hemisphere started almost immediately to outline its future destiny. Through commerce conducted primarily in Boston, New York, and Philadelphia, trade began to create wealth in a fantastic growth. Eli Whitney, a Yankee schoolteacher living in Georgia, invented a machine that enabled one man to seed one hundred pounds of cotton a day instead of the single pound that could have been seeded before this invention. And almost simultaneously Samuel Slater, in Massachusetts, built the first American spinning machine. Thus developed the first new wealth of the American agricultural society, and the foundations for a new industrial one.

If these developments seem remote from the story of the White House, remember that up to this time there was no mass agriculture or basic industry in the country, with the exception of tobacco. Wealth was required to carry out the great projects dreamed of by the country's leaders—consolidation of the continent's interest in the hands of the new government and a proper stance *vis-à-vis* the strife-torn European countries that looked for advantages in the Western Hemisphere.

When Jefferson and Madison looked at the maps and charts of this United States, they studied a country that was large but was hemmed in by strong and ambitious foreign powers.

The northern border was held by Britain, still rankling over the Revolution and even more disturbed over the swings in alliances that might affect its war with France. France held most of the surveyed area of the United States west of the Mississippi River. Spain had old and established forces in Florida. Even the Mediterranean provoked Jefferson's new Administration, with Tripoli formally declaring war on the country in June 1801 because of American refusal to pay tribute to it, in the form of protection money for commercial activity.

It took four years to win the war with Tripoli, but in that period American naval action increased the country's prestige in Europe, while Jefferson—no longer enamored of the French revolutionaries—steered a course of neutrality between France and Britain.

When war broke out between Napoleon's government and Great Britain in 1803, Jefferson, with the help of James Monroe and Madison, brought about the first major coup in the country's expansion. The precedent he set for the White House was an important one—that the President conducts foreign negotiations on his own responsibility; whatever actions may be constitutionally required by Congress come later.

Jefferson and Madison sent Monroe to Paris in 1803 with an offer to purchase from France the city of New Orleans and West Florida at a price not to exceed $10,000,000. The real estate may not have been worth much, but such a deal would assure United States control of the mouth of the Mississippi River and clear away any threat to control of the Gulf of Mexico that might develop in Florida. Monroe was instructed to act with Robert Livingston, Minister to France, who had re-established good relations there.

To the surprise of the negotiators, Napolion wanted more but was willing to give more—much more. He offered to cede the entire Louisiana Territory for $11,250,000 in American bonds if in addition the United States would assume claims by American citizens against France totaling $3,750,000. The deal was concluded on that basis. For a little while, the prestige of the White House and prosperity of the nation soared high, and in the following year Jefferson was overwhelmingly re-elected.

There came again opportunity for developing the grace and charm of life in the mansion. And the city began to show substantial development, although its growth was very slow. It continued to be more a seat for country gentlemen than a metropolis.

Paradoxically Jefferson tried to make the White House a showcase of democracy, at the same time demanding good food, good wines, and tasteful activities. Jefferson prided himself on being a "plain" person, but his accounts recorded $10,000 spent for wines in his eight years in office. He ruled out the formal "levee" that marked palace receptions of that day in Europe, but he constantly held receptions. He canceled the custom of having ladies escorted into the dining room, each by a partner according to protocol (to the dismay of Mrs. Merry, wife of the British minister), but he brought twelve house servants from Monticello to prepare and handle these affairs.

As a hobby, to exercise one of his many talents, Jefferson had terraces constructed on the east and west sides of the mansion, plus a little garden house that he used as a private office. With Hoban and Latrobe he spent hours over the original plans on which the building had been constructed, working out designs for the north and south porticoes that would be added in the future. As the grounds gradually were landscaped he personally directed the planting of elms and magnolias. Some of these have survived to the present time.

Also, Jefferson's many other interests set a pattern for American living that spread and grew in what had been predominantly a trading and farming society. To amuse his friends he would play his violin, or proudly display his always growing collection of fossils, plants, and minerals. He drafted a design for a new type of plow and wrote a booklet on the virtues of crop rotation. When William Clark, his private secretary, and Meriwether Lewis broached their idea to explore the Northwest Territory, he adopted it as a pet project and saw them on their way in 1804.

Under such stimulus Washington began to assume at least the intellectual character of a national capital, although it had no paved streets, no sewers, no central water supply and no street lighting. The Potomac River almost washed the foundations of the southern side of the mansion, and game was still plentiful within the limits of the city.

Under the stimulus of Jefferson—and, to some degree, Dolley Madison—a recognizable Washington "society" developed. Upon visiting Washington, the author Washington Irving noted that Dolley Madison "is a fine, portly, buxom dame, who has a smile and a pleasant word for everybody." And he added, "But as for Jemmy Madison—Ah! Poor Jemmy!—he is but a withered little Apple-John."

In 1804 the mansion was a center of interest in other unrelated events that kept building more and more precedents. Old animosities were dramatically recalled when Aaron Burr killed Alexander Hamilton in their famous duel; Martha Jefferson Randolph, the President's only daughter, gave the first White House debut for her own daughter Ann, after moving in with her father in 1804, and in the same year gave birth to another child, who was christened James Madison Randolph.

Controversy flared with Spain over Florida, and the British began "pressing" American seamen in their urgency to fight the French. Early in 1808 Jefferson again enlarged the authority of the Presidency when he declared (and made it stick) an embargo on American shipping to avoid further involvement in the British-French War. Yet despite the protests from badly hurt merchants he saw James Madison easily win election as his successor, almost exclusively on his recommendation, and despite a contest launched by Monroe.

Three days before Madison's Inaugural Jefferson repealed the embargo on shipping. He sat in a box as guest of honor at the Inauguration Ball. A week later, riding at the head of a string of wagons carrying his personal effects, Jefferson returned to Monticello, his "elysium of domestic affections," and, like John Adams, never again returned to Washington.

Nevertheless, Jefferson left behind precedents for the conduct of the Presidency that remained durable and constant, some of them running counter to his younger and more revolutionary ideas. A strong advocate of States' rights, he began the great centralization of power in the Presidency. An isolationist in feeling, he expanded both the borders of his country and its foreign commitments. As a "democrat" politically he left a stamp of luxury and culture on its atmosphere.

Now, in 1808, just as John Adams' Administration had been principally the political extension of George Washington's, Madison became the residuary legatee of Jeffersonian policies. Until the outbreak of the War of 1812, his Administration was a placid one; no drama would occur until the invasion of Washington by the British in 1814.

Madison dutifully tended to his job, and in his scholarly manner emulated some of the habits of Jefferson's peacetime Administration. In the mansion's story it was his destiny to take second place.

Dolley Madison saving the Declaration of Independence, 1814. Drawn by Benjamin West Clinedinst

She signed her name "D. P. Madison," was reared in a Quaker household, and no hint of scandal ever threw an aura of mysterious romance around her. But Dolley Madison created a period in the White House and in the United States that is as yet unmatched—with the possible exception of the era of the Kennedys.

A plain and relatively plump housewife, Dolley Madison is shown in a prized engraving owned by the Library of Congress dressed in a dark gown with an Elizabethan collar, with a fringed brocaded shawl over her shoulders and on her head a large turban with tassels, which became her favorite type of headgear in maturity.

In 1808 she was forty-one years old, and married for fifteen of these to James Madison, whom she overshadowed in every respect except for intellect and political skill. Her husband was fifty-eight.

As mistress of the White House, Dolley Madison sat at the head of the dinner table, entertained prodigiously and took snuff from a lacquered box, to the discomfort of her female friends. But her friendships became enduring, and her generosity was reportedly unmatched. Once she gave twenty dollars and a cow to a benefit for orphans.

When she died at the age of eighty-one, she had become the dearest friend of the younger but also aging Daniel Webster, who directed his servant to smuggle hampers of food from his kitchen into hers to conceal from Dolley the poverty into which she had fallen.

Her grand career followed romance and tragedy in earlier years that might well have consigned a less attractive (or less ambitious?) woman to the veiled anonymity of widows of this period.

Born in North Carolina and reared in Virginia, with the family name of Payne, the young Dolley went to Philadelphia with her widowed mother, who opened a boardinghouse to cater to the officials in the temporary Capital of the United States. There she married John Todd, Jr., a rising lawyer and a relatively wealthy young man. In the ensuing three years she bore him one son and in August 1793 was again pregnant. That August a plague of yellow fever struck the city and continued until curtailed by cold weather in November. In the meantime it took the lives of one-sixth of the population.

Todd might have taken his family to some distant and healthy place, and sat out the plague, but he lived up to the best Quaker tradition: he sent Dolley and his son to the healthy region near Grey's Ferry, Pennsylvania, and turned to duty as a volunteer nurse. After long and exhausting work, Todd went to join his wife for a brief rest. But he already had caught the fever, and Dolley nursed him until it struck her. When she recovered she learned that her husband had died. So in the winter, with her children, she returned to Philadelphia and her mother's house, and soon became active again in the social life of Philadelphia.

In the camaraderie of politics in 1793,

during George Washington's early years in the Presidency, many men who later would become partisan enemies were still close friends. Two of these were Madison and Aaron Burr. Burr knew the widow Todd; some reports have it that he was living at Mrs. Payne's boardinghouse. Madison, after seeing Dolley about town, asked Burr to arrange an introduction, and one evening Burr took his friend to call formally on her. Dolley received them in her mother's sitting room, wearing a mulberry silk dress and with a tulle handkerchief tied over her curls. For a fourth, she had invited Miss Elizabeth Collins Lee to join them.

Madison and Dolley were married in September 1794 after the bride had been a widow for a year, and she thereby became hostess for her husband in his position as a member of Congress from Virginia. Two years later, reflecting Jefferson's dislike for the handling of government by the Federalists, Madison took his family to his estate at Montpelier to pursue the life of a country gentleman and promote scientific farming.

The plan sounded good, but the political quarrels that engaged Jefferson under John Adams prompted Madison to rejoin him; then upon Jefferson's Inauguration Madison came to Washington as Secretary of State. And without apparent effort or ambition Dolley Madison came to be White House hostess eight years before her husband was elected President and she became mistress of the mansion in her own right.

For the first time the President's mansion represented a booming, prosperous,

44

and optimistic United States on the way to its assumed great destiny.

The shipping embargo was ended, and American vessels again were spreading their sails on journeys to all parts of the commercial world. Property suddenly boomed in value, and otherwise cautious men began investing in speculative ventures in the west opened up by the Louisiana Purchase and the opportunities reported by Lewis and Clark.

The Congress gave Dolley Madison an appropriation of $6000 to freshen up the White House, which she spent and carefully recorded in the account books: $458 for a piano and $28 for a guitar. Yellow satin was used to reupholster much of the furniture, and satin damask draperies were made for some of the tall windows. Mirrors were installed over the mantelpieces.

At this point only the decorative touches such as these seemed to have been necessary, since Jefferson had taken care of the architectural details, such as installing bells that worked, and completing the main reception rooms. The house now was occasionally referred to—seriously and not in levity—as the "palace."

Dolley Madison took every opportunity to show that the White House's inhabitants were, insofar as social things could demonstrate, the wealthy master and mistress of a palace. The President's salary was $25,000 a year, which was no pittance, but an income that seemed insufficient for Madison's predecessor and his successors. Madison did die bankrupt some years later, but for the moment, in their manner of living, he and Dolley seemed wealthy indeed.

This was an era in the United States when the poor could get by on what seem by modern values to be an incredibly small amount of money. At the other extreme, luxuries enjoyed by the rich were incredibly dear. One recalls a reference in George Washington's accounts to his commissioning a ship's captain bound for England to spend $500 for the cloth for a new gown for Martha Washington, and accessories to go with it. Some economists reckon dollars in the early nineteenth century as having ten times the purchasing power of mid-twentieth-century American currency. This helps to point up Dolley Madison's flurry of spending when for $1500 she bought a new coach in which to make her social rounds. And what rounds they were!

It long has been a legend that no White House hostess has entertained as much or as lavishly as Mrs. Madison. Perhaps that is true, on a marathon basis, despite the relatively small size of the National Capital and the official and social set to entertain and to be entertained.

For the entertaining, the Madisons procured a dinner service of blue Lowestoft china, to replace the Cantonese porcelain that Jefferson had set before his dinner guests. Dolley Madison had overcome her family's Quaker scruples against using slaves, and recorded the purchase of one for her own account, at a price of $400 with the condition that the slave should be freed after five years. As for clothes, she spent $2000 for a single lot from Paris.

Unfortunately there is no known record of the cost of candles for the house's chandeliers, whose requirements had so frightened Abigail Adams, but this luxury item must have been enormous. And over the entertainments of the White House presided a person representing the ultimate touch in the new cosmopolitan social life —a French steward, Jean Pierre Sioussat, nicknamed "French Jean."

From an earlier account comes this description as the Madisons took over:

The mansion flourished in precise relationship to a quickening in the pulse of the nation for the country was getting the feel of itself. A lush birthrate provided a steady increase in population despite a slackening in immigration due to the wars abroad. People were going westward in a steady stream, to new prosperity, and the industrial East prospered with this prosperity, although Southern planters became less wealthy.

American commerce flowed in a steady stream westward into the new country, down the Ohio and the Mississippi, between the seaports of the East and the newly acquired metropolis of New Orleans.

America felt the first flush of wholesale development, a sudden awareness that the country really was something. It was proud, loud, and not overly sympathetic toward the gentle and the refined. It liked its food served on plate, but the food must be solid, substantial. It liked its clothes to be the best procurable, but it wore them over shoulders broader than English ones. It spoke the King's English, but with an accent that already differentiated widely the two English-speaking races.

Although never a visitor to Europe, Dolley Madison created a sort of "court" in the President's palace, made its social life a mirror of the politics and temper of the times and worked hard to elevate the dignity of the Presidency; yet in all ways possible she maintained the democratic forms of the day.

The holidays in the summer months must have been as necessary for the women in official circles as for the men. *45*

From fall through spring, Washington gave outdoors the impression of a hazy, lazy, sprawling Southern town without any of the amenities of other cities—not yet even a constable to patrol the streets' numerous "shanty towns" still occupied by squatters left over from the first construction days. Here and there were fine new houses surrounded by stables, gardens, slave quarters, and other outbuildings. These houses were growing in number, slowly but impressively.

Taking the District of Columbia as a whole, grand new houses began to cap some of the hills, two of them—Arlington in Virginia and Tudor Place in Georgetown financed from the legacies left by Martha Washington. Georgetown's quota of mansions increased.

Pennsylvania Avenue, along the mile with which it connected with White House and the Capitol might be dusty or muddy according to the season, but it was lined with elm trees that had been planted by Jefferson. Near the Capitol were wooden sidewalks in front of shops that housed tailors, men's hairdressers and wigmakers, and related services.

In a female world as yet undimmed by the later idiosyncracies of Queen Victoria, Dolley Madison led the way in wearing disconcertingly revealing clothes. Women's bosoms were exposed to the lowest possible V-point; shoulders were bare and gowns lavish in their full skirts and trains. Hair was worn in the extreme heights of French coiffures. Sometimes, a question is asked as to how the ladies of American cities simultaneously wore the French fashions, when it was not always possible or affordable for them to have clothes consigned to them. The answer was first given through the custom of engravers in Paris and London making up lithographs that could be copied by clever seamstresses. Soon, by Dolley Madison's time in the White House, enterprising French dollmakers were clothing these little manikins in authentic styles, not for destructive play in childish hands but as detailed models to be copied in adult clothing.

Foreign missions began to take root in Washington, adding their uniforms to the color of social life at about the time that the Jefferson influence was dulling the male plumage of American officials. Yet old-timers like President Madison still donned satin knee breeches, white silk stockings, and pumps with jeweled buckles for formal attire.

The year 1808 marked the advent of Washington's brightest bird of plumage. As a gesture toward healing old wounds after Jefferson lifted the blockade, Emperor Napoleon sent as Minister to Washington, General Turreau de Garambonville, Marshal of France. No particular record remains of the work of the Marshal as a diplomat, but diaries and writings of the period glisten with words—mostly superlatives—attempting to describe his plumes, his gold lace, and the diamond-studded orders which he wore.

Also, the magnet of the Capital's life was drawing more and more of the varied talented Americans to Washington, including a new generation of statesmen with fire and vision, who will figure somewhat later in this account, but also men who came on missions and often stayed.

There was Robert Smith, described as "a man of wealth and fashion," who was

From an original Sketch taken on the spot by C.W. Janson, Esq.

The President's House in Washington; (lately taken & destroyed by the British Army)

Published Nov. 1st 1814. by G & S. Robinson, Paternoster Row.

Sketch by C. W. Janson of White House, which appeared in Lady's Magazine, *1814*

called to Washington in 1804 to become Jefferson's Secretary of the Navy, and who remained as Madison's Secretary of State.

John Peter Van Ness, a New York patroon, went to Washington as a member of Congress, and within a year married the local heiress and beauty Marcia Burns. He built a large house designed by Latrobe, retired from Congress, and settled importantly into local life as major of the local militia.

Joel Barlow, better known now for his poetry, including the verse immortalizing hasty pudding, was a celebrated early American diplomat somewhat outside the political circles. His fortune was large enough to permit him to become the first of a long line of American career officials who have combined literature and diplom-

acy as life occupations. In fact, Barlow's wealth was such that Mrs. Samuel Smith noted in her diary that he had stopped on one mission at the boardinghouse run by a Mrs. Doyne where he paid the large weekly rate of forty dollars for his and Mrs. Barlow's accommodations, plus that for two servants and stabling of their horses. Barlow settled finally in a pretentious estate named Kalorama about a mile and a half from the White House.

Barlow was noted for more than just his poetry. He was another of the legion of forgotten heroes of the early days. He first obtained distinction as American Consul to Algiers, where he obtained the release of many sailors captured by the Barbary pirates. He died of exposure on the plains of eastern Europe in a mission to seek out   *47*

Napoleon when the emperor was in the midst of his retreat from Moscow.

These few were typical of the social "court" members for whom Dolley Madison set the customs of the day and whom she entertained lavishly at weekly formal receptions, frequent balls, suppers followed by card games, of which the most popular with the women was loo. Dolley's constitution must have been an iron one, because every lady new to Washington left calling cards at the White House, and she made one small bit of her reputation by meticulously returning every call—sometimes fifteen in a day. Of course, the visiting and card-leaving had to be repeated at the beginning of each fall season.

An "outside look" into this developing and typical Washington society is given in the notes of Sir Augustus Foster, an attaché of the British Legation who was sent to the Capital while Jefferson was still President. He stated some of his dislikes of Washington, particularly the extremes of climate, but found it agreeable and, to his shrewd eyes, interesting:

There were a number of rich proprieters in the State of Maryland. In the district around Washington, I was assured there were 500 persons possessing estates which returned them an income of 1,000 pounds. Mr. Lloyd, a member of Congress on the Eastern Branch [a tributary of the Potomac], possessed a net revenue of between six and seven thousand pounds, with which he had only to buy clothes for himself and his family, wine, equipage, furniture and other luxuries. Mr. Tayloe also, whose whole income exceeded 15,000 pounds per annum, held 3,000 acres of land which his father had bought for 500 pounds. He possessed 500 slaves, built brigs and schooners, worked iron mines, converted the iron into ploughshares—

and all this was done by the hands of his own subjects.

Not many members of the Congress were in evidence socially, according to Sir Augustus, but nowhere had he seen prettier girls, or more of them. Yet the men far outnumbered the girls, which cut down the necessity for these belles to exert themselves.

As there were but few of them, however, in proportion to the great number of men who frequented the places of amusement in the Federal City, it is one of the most marrying places in the whole continent—a truth which was beginning to be found out and became by and by the cause of vast numbers flocking thither, all around from the four points of the compass. Maugre the march of intellect so much vaunted in the present century, the literary education of these ladies is far from being worthy of the age of knowledge, and conversation is apt to flag, though a seat by the ladies is much coveted.

Dancing and music served to eke out the time, but one got to be heartily sick of hearing the same song everywhere, even when it was, "Just Like Love Is Yonder Rose." No matter how this was sung, the words alone were the man-traps; the belle of the evening was declared to be just like both—and people looked around as if the listener was expected to become on the instant very tender and propose—and sometimes such a result does in reality take place; both parties when betrothed use a great deal of billing and cooing. . . .

In going to assemblies one had sometimes to drive three or four miles within the city bounds, and very often at the great risk of overturn, or being what is called "stalled," or stuck in the mud, when one can neither get backward nor forward, and either loses one's shoes or one's patience. . . . Cards were a great resource of an evening, and gaming was all the fashion, at brag, especially, for the men who frequented society, who were chiefly from Virginia, or the Western States, and were very fond of this, the most gambling of all games. Loo was the innocent diversion of the ladies,

48

who when they were "looed" pronounced the word in a very mincing manner.

Although the formalities of government were time-consuming, Washington rapidly gathered around the White House activities common in other American and European cities. In summer and fall there was racing at the National Race Course, featuring heavy betting and attention-getting gowns worn by the ladies. Theater troupes prospered, and when Congress was in session, the debates were heavily attended.

The Capitol was not much to see as yet, its completion having been outstripped by the White House, but chambers were finished for the House and Senate—small ones that now are only anterooms in the massive building. Where now the dome stands was an open space. As in European parliaments, sessions were held in the evening after early dinners.

There the oratory and the company both were on a high plane. In 1810 John C. Calhoun and Henry Clay won seats in Congress, as members of the fiery younger generation of patriots. Both were skilled orators and hard political fighters, capable of filling the galleries when it was known that either would speak.

Dolley Madison entertained her closest friends in the small gallery reserved for the President, close by another where diplomats and foreign guests could bow to or exchange conversation with her.

Despite the well-fed condition of the gallery visitors, who had customarily finished their large dinners at about four o'clock, servants thoughtfully provided hampers of food which, often as not, contained some specially wrapped portions to be lowered from the railings to hungry friends on the floors of the Senate and House. As yet, the Congress had no private restaurant, but the cloakrooms were well stocked with liquid refreshments.

There is no record that Dolley Madison ever stepped over the line from her social position in the White House to the field of politics and policy, but she played an unusually important role of confidante, companion, and background arranger for her retiring and harassed husband. Even diplomacy had to be practiced assiduously in the realm of domestic politics, for there were sharp divisions arising between the North and the South, on the basis of different economic interests. And the South itself was not unified. Tensions were also caused by Monroe's unsuccessful bid to defeat Madison for the Presidency. It took three years to heal this breach, when Madison made Monroe his Secretary of State and, for periods of 1813–14, simultaneously Secretary of War.

Long before Madison's re-election to a second term in November of 1812, lights were burning late in the President's study; couriers were riding constantly between the centers of population, principally carrying out reports and returning with reports of public opinion on the growing crisis with England.

Such activities wrote the finale to the first phase of the Dolley Madison era, and normally would conclude with her quiet withdrawal into a woman's world. However, Dolley would write another chapter in our national history.

A VIEW of the PRESIDENTS HOUSE in the CITY of WASHINGTON
after the Conflagration of the 24th August 1814.

The White House after being burned by the British, 1814

Invasion and Ruin 6

In the months when Madison was finishing his first term in the White House, he found himself in a crisis the like of which no previous President had faced. The responsibilities suddenly thrust upon the White House were minor compared with those of today, but the scope of Presidential leadership was indeed broadened.

War was threatening the United States. As usual, no thoughtful leaders wanted war. Business was opposed to war, particularly the wealthy trading centers. Most of all among these, Madison wished so strongly to avert war that he was accused of timidity.

Yet the demands on the White House were for many acts and policy decisions that could lead to war. Fiery Henry Clay spoke so bluntly that his followers became known as the War Hawks. And on the other side, those who opposed war accused the War Hawks of what would be called "brinkmanship" today.

The British Navy again was impressing seamen, or kidnaping from American ships at sea those sailors who could not prove—and few could—that they were Americans not of British origin. British forces in eastern Canada were viewed as a hostile threat, and British authority in the Northwest was resented by trappers, traders, and would-be settlers. Each interested element implored the President to do something, but peacefully.

Madison felt very much alone in this period. He was not a pugnacious man, and his brilliance was a brilliance of thought and writing, not of oratory or military strategy. Because of his indecision he went down to Monticello—a long and arduous trip by coach—to talk over his problems with Thomas Jefferson, but apparently got little advice or comfort. More alone than ever he returned to the growing pressures for militant action against England pounding against the White House walls.

Madison asked Congress to vote a declaration of war on England, primarily because of England's enforcement of a blockade of France, on June 1, 1812. Over the opposition of the New England States, the declaration was passed by Congress—ironically, as it turned out (at least, so it appears in the twentieth century with our almost instant international communications) because it was learned only later that the blockade had been ordered raised.

Now Madison, as Constitutional Commander-in-Chief of the country's forces in wartime, was voted by Congress an army of 44,500 men and a navy of twenty major ships mounting five hundred guns. For two years the war continued, with its minor successes and minor defeats, reflected at the White House principally in dispatches recounting the relatively small pressure being applied by England and the small but heroic deeds of some Americans.

Then there occurred one of the most shameful and useless acts of wanton destruction ever perpetrated by a modern and presumably civilized army. . . . Perhaps it was due to the severity of the August heat in Washington; in any event, the undefended Capitol and White House were burned.

Suddenly the National Capital, going through the actions of preparing for war, found that war was on its doorstep. On August 22, 1814, messengers brought word that a force of four thousand British soldiers, commanded by General Robert Ross, had landed on the banks of the Potomac below Washington from a fleet commanded by Admiral Sir George Cockburn.

Some fled Washington, others heard that the British had announced that they planned to capture the city but that no citizen would be hurt or his property damaged if he kept to his house and offered no resistance.

The militia that had been drilling at intervals for two years mustered in Bladensburg a total of some five thousand men, many armed with hunting guns, only a few with uniforms. One of their officers was James Monroe, not as a Cabinet member but as a colonel in the motley group. He rode with the President when Madison went out early on the morning of the twenty-fourth to review this "home guard," to talk with the men, and to inspect the city's defenses.

About the only substantial defense was a battery of Navy guns taken by Captain Joshua Barney and placed astride the Bladensburg Road, which the British must use to enter Washington.

For White House security, Madison had it surrounded by a guard of one hundred picked soldiers under the command of Captain Daniel Carroll. But if in fact there turned out to be a commander in the White House that day it was Dolley Madison.

The "battle" of Bladensburg was hardly even a skirmish as the British regulars overran the panicky militiamen. Captain Barney's Navy detail fired its guns until they were overrun—most were killed. Then, in parade formation, the invaders moved into the city, undeterred by American reinforcements including Captain Carroll's men.

First they paused to burn the Capitol, and since the day was windy sparks from this fire soon spread to many houses adjoining it. These useless fires, in a city no longer defended or a threat to the British, caused a panic as refugees streamed west and clogged the bridge over the Potomac from Washington to Arlington, Virginia.

This became Dolley Madison's hour and, with an uncanny sense of historic timing, she simultaneously did what the heroine of such a story should do and reported it in a letter written in bits and pieces through the day. The letter to a sister, Lucy, was sent off by an unnamed messenger, after she had packed important papers to take with her and with feminine thoroughness locked the doors of the White House.

Dawn found Dolley Madison on the roof of the building "turning my spyglass in every direction," and reporting that "alas, I can decry only groups of military wandering in all directions, as if there were a lack of arms or spirit to fight for their own firesides."

Then she went to work: "I have pressed as many Cabinet papers into trunks as to fill one carriage; our private property must be sacrificed, as it is impossible to procure wagons for its transportation."

She wrote that French Jean had suggested that they blow up the White House, but that was beyond Dolley Madison's imagination or ability.

Three o'clock.—Will you believe it, my sister? We have had a battle, or skirmish, near Bladensburg, and I am still here within sound of the cannon! Mr. Madison comes not, may God protect him! Two messengers covered with dust, come to bid me fly; but I wait for him. . . . At this late hour a wagon has been procured; and I have had it filled with the plate and most valuable portraits belonging to the house; whether it will reach its destination, the Bank of Maryland, or fall into the hands of British soldiers, events must determine.

Our kind friend, Mr. Carroll, has come to hasten my departure, and is in a very bad humor with me because I insist on waiting until the large picture of General Washington is secured, and it requires to be unscrewed from the wall. This process has been found too tedious for these perilous moments; I have ordered the frame to be broken and the canvas to be taken out; it is done—and the precious portrait has been placed in the hands of two gentlemen from New York for safekeeping. And now, dear sister, I must leave this house, or the retreating army will make me a prisoner in it, by filling up the road I am directed to take. When I shall write to you, or where I shall be tomorrow, I cannot tell!

Dolley Madison's coachman put the last crowded bits of luggage into her carriage. French Jean took her parrot in its cage around to Octagon House before departing for Philadelphia, and the President's wife joined the stream of refugees riding or running toward Georgetown and the bridge to Virginia. There on the following day Madison joined her at an unnamed rendezvous spot, and together they started to pick up the pieces of the Government.

In the meantime, the British forces, after setting fire to the Capitol, went leisurely to the White House. There the men held a party, drinking the wines from the cellar, and then set the building afire. Its well-seasoned beams and paneling burned briskly, into the night until a rainstorm quenched the flames, but only after the walls had been left a blackened ruin.

Then the invaders set off for Baltimore, perhaps too confident of their easy victory. The Maryland troops drove back the British, and in their battles General Ross was killed.

Madison returned to the Capital four days after the debacle, to begin reconstruction of the staff of the Government, and the Congress began to assemble, although it officially was still in recess. At first, the great question was what the country would think of the Capital, and of the White House as its seat of government. But within days of the event, it was agreed that Washington must continue to be the Capital, and a certain national pride began to be manifested in the decision.

In the odd and unexpected turns of history, and perhaps to a large degree because of the manner in which the Madisons had deported themselves, in the eyes of the people the White House grew in stature—and in the respect the people held for it.

Madison returned to Washington late on Friday or early Saturday, and sent to Dolley in her Virginia refuge a note to rejoin him. Like many another husband who has had to find a new location, he wrote to her: "I know not where we are in the first instance to hide our heads, but shall look for a place upon your arrival." *53*

The problem of hiding their heads, and reconstituting a temporary Presidential headquarters was solved by a neighbor, the owner of Octagon House. They joined their parrot in its refuge, while the Congress took over the Patent Office as its meeting place. From Monticello the aging Jefferson sent a note applauding the decision to retain Washington as the capital city.

Through the following months, problems piled so high as to diminish the burning of the Capital's principal buildings. The war planners asked for $50,-000,000 to pursue the conflict for another year, over and above the prospective $24,000,000 expected from normal revenues. Massachusetts, Connecticut, and Rhode Island threatened under the Hartford Convention to secede from the Union. In his masterly capacity for understatement, Monroe said in a message to Congress, "It is not to be disguised that the situation of our country calls for its greatest effort."

And William Wirt, lawyer and author, left a summarizing commentary on the whole dreary mess:

> I went to look at the ruins of the President's House. The rooms which you saw so richly furnished, exhibited nothing but unroofed, naked walls, cracked, defaced and blackened with fire. I cannot tell you what I felt as I walked among them. . . . I called on the President. He looks miserably shattered and woebegone. In short, he looks heartbroken. His mind is full of the New England sedition. He introduced the subject, and continued to press it— painful as it obviously was to him. I denied the probability, even the *possibility*, that the yeomanry of the North could be induced to place themselves under the power and protection of England, and diverted the conversation to another topic; but he took the first opportunity to return to it, and convinced me that his heart and mind were painfully full of the subject.

In the following months James Monroe grew into the political maturity that was to lead him to the Presidency. While he served simultaneously as Secretary of State and War, he substituted for Secretary of the Treasury Gallatin when the latter headed a mission to Ghent, which was working on a peaceful settlement of the war.

Octagon House became the first of periodic temporary White Houses. Hoban got out his old plans for the White House and began surveying the needs for reconstruction. Word of the peace treaty signed at Ghent on December 24 reached Washington, carried by another Carroll, Henry, on February 4, and Madison became the country's hero. Carroll took it to Madison in his second-floor study at Octagon House, and then shouted the news from the gallery of the staircase to Dolley and a group of friends gathered below.

With the Congress and the country in a happier mood, the President was able to appropriate funds to begin immediate reconstruction of the Capitol and the White House. For the remaining two years of his term, Madison lived in Octagon House while Hoban, now with sufficient financial backing, reconstructed the White House. Dr. Thornton again advanced his earlier suggestion that porticoes be erected at the north and south sides, but economic restraints still ruled them out.

Monroe was elected President in 1816, and Dolley Madison, already the country's most notable woman, accompanied

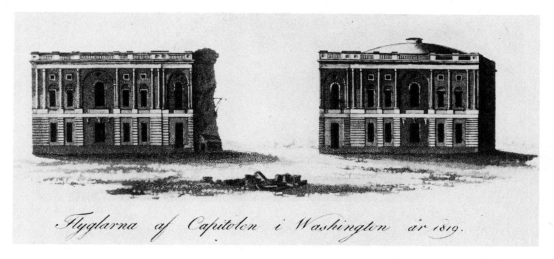

Flyglarna af Capitolen i Washington år 1819.

her husband to Montpelier, where she lived until his death in 1836. The Executive Mansion passed to other hands, new customs, and took on a new personality. The White House was reopened in the fall of 1818, its newly painted white walls giving it its permanent name.

At the conclusion of Madison's term, the Virginia Dynasty would continue for another eight years, but the modifications in Government and in power continued to enrich and enlarge the prestige of Washington's central emblem, the White House.

The War of 1812, as small and as un-necessary as it possibly was, had nonetheless elevated the nation to a major power in world affairs. England had been defeated, and the United States had been the victor—not as a group of colonies in rebellion but as an independent nation.

Madison had been a strong President and his wife had set the pattern for a special leadership among women. As the White House and the Capitol again rose from their foundations, the Madisons prepared for the transition between Administrations, with Madison taking every opportunity to indicate his preference for Monroe.

55

Placque purchased by Monroe

In December of 1817 the rebuilding of the White House was completed. The Monroes moved into the building in an atmosphere that overnight relegated even Dolley Madison and her recent era to a legendary past.

The master of the house belonged to a generation to whom the Revolution was a boyhood experience: he had left the College of William and Mary at the age of eighteen to enlist. The mistress of the house was of British nationality, daughter of an officer of the English Army who had been part of the occupation forces in New York City in the Revolution. Both husband and wife, as the result of long missions abroad, were cosmopolites.

To Monroe, his birthplace in Westmoreland County, Virginia, was simply a sentimental memory, and his modest new home, Ash Lawn, near Charlottesville and overlooking Monticello, was simply a country retreat that eventually he would sell when he made his permanent residence in New York City. In the Presidency, Monroe was the last of the "Virginia gentlemen," and in his personal attitude he divorced himself from that background to typify the new Americanism. To cap the sweep of change, Monroe in 1817 named as his Secretary of State John Quincy Adams, son of President John Adams and the first Yankee to return to high position in Washington since his father's Administration.

While Monroe's election to the Presidency had been fought out in a bitter struggle between American political factions—and he himself was called by critics "James the Lesser"—the White House became an international symbol of government among capitals that might be larger but which held it in respect. Much of Europe had a stake in the good will of the White House, where friendship had swung back toward France.

Hyde de Neuville was the new Minister from France, and he vied for leadership of the Diplomatic Corps with Sir Charles Bagot of Great Britain. Both now could meet on friendly terms at White House dinners, which sparkled with the color and uniforms of a distinguished list of foreign dignitaries: Luis de Onis, Minister of Spain; Abbé José Correa da Serra, witty elderly crony of Jefferson and now Portuguese Minister from the exiled government established in Brazil, and Baron Johan Albert de Kantzov, Minister Resident of Sweden and Norway.

The European diplomats waltzed through punctilio and paid court to the White House, while adding to its color, and each had his own kettle of fish to fry. But these diplomats were not the only influences on the new political atmosphere, for America was developing its own colorful personalities. General William Harrison was invited to more dinners than he could eat, and James Brown, Senator from Louisiana, was one of the most prodigious entertainers, as he angled for his goal, the post of Minister to France. Commodore Stephen Decatur

George Catlin drawing of north façade, 1820

commissioned Latrobe to build a new house for him and his wife opposite the northwest corner of the White House grounds.

And in this melee, Elizabeth Kortwright Monroe quietly revolutionized White House social life in a manner that drew scathing criticism upon her, but which stuck forever afterward. She set apart from all other practices the role of the First Lady, even at the price of being castigated as a snob, while admired in other ways for her taste and official tact.

Mrs. Monroe, tiny and delicate in contrast to Dolley Madison, created her private furor immediately after Monroe was inaugurated. She laid down the rule that the wife of the President would receive callers, but would not return calls.

From current descriptions of the Washington of that period, there is little wonder that she refused to follow the pattern of the more robust Dolley Madison. There were as yet no paved streets, no sewers, and no police or sanitary corps. John Randolph of Roanoke publicly described Pennsylvania Avenue as "the great Serbonian bog," and Monroe himself called the city a "sheep walk." Abbé Serra, noted as a wit, made a play on L'Enfant's vision of this "city of magnificent vistas" by dubbing it "the city of magnificent distances."

And through all the streets, which haphazardly connected clusters of houses, ran cattle and hogs. Slops were thrown into

Painting of White House with porticoes finally finished, 1826

the streets from the houses, and only rains washed into gullies the droppings of horses. Even the White House grounds were ill defined, but the interior of the restored mansion helped somewhat to make up for the outward lacks.

As restoration of the structure progressed, the Congress appropriated in a single sum $50,000 to pay for its refurnishing. This was in 1817 a lavish sum of money and the First Lady was not yet hampered by limitations on how it was to be spent.

Mrs. Monroe ordered the new White House furnishings from France in the era now considered one of the finest in furniture design. Chairs, sofas, and commodes reflected that taste. The new dinner serv-

ice was thin white French china bordered in orange, and another French chef—not remembered now by name as was French Jean—was imported to manage the kitchens.

The furor over not returning calls died down after Elizabeth Monroe established a routine of open hospitality in which she received all of her social callers with special grace, laid out an extensive program of formal dinners and receptions, and once a week threw open the doors of the mansion to all who cared to drop in.

But—and the exception was important —at the first reception marking reopening of the White House she nearly undid all the good will established during her and the President's temporary stay at Octagon 59

Minerva clock and two candelabra typical of the elegant Monroe era

Fireplace of the State Dining Room

Strollers on Pennsylvania Avenue in 1826

Drawing by Madame Hyde de Neuville, wife of the French Minister, 1820

PRESIDENTS HOUSE.

Engraving by August Köllner, 1820s

House. Callers gasped when they entered the East Room.

There they saw their hostess, toying with a tortoise-shell lorgnette, her hair dressed high and topped with feathers, seated on a raised platform to which the callers were escorted to make their bows. The raised platform, reminiscent of thrones, made its moment of sensational history, and then disappeared. It really was difficult for feuds or ruffled tempers to last very long in the atmosphere that caused this period to be termed "the era of good feelings."

Neither a strong leader nor a hero, Monroe got along well in his political affairs and thereby enhanced the prestige of the White House, holding the support alike of Henry Clay and the fiery new Senator John C. Calhoun.

While he supported Andrew Jackson's foray into Florida with an army to prevent Indians and their alleged Spanish supporters from raiding Georgia, he worked out a deal to "buy" for $5,000,000 this Spanish possession and settled a border dispute over Texas, then part of Mexico, by confirming the Sabine River as the boundary between Louisiana and Texas.

This same President increased American prestige overseas, without fighting further wars, but in a manner that caused flurries in foreign chancelleries. Liberia was established as an independent country on the west coast of Africa—its independence forever guaranteed by the United States—as a homeland to which freed slaves might return, and the country's new capital was named Monrovia.

More important, and with more risk, Monroe through John Quincy Adams notified the world powers that the fu-ture freedom of the Western Hemisphere would thereafter be the direct concern of the United States. In this Monroe Doctrine, warning was bluntly given that the republic would fight off, if necessary, any further attempts to colonize or to overthrow established American governments by foreign powers.

Under such leadership the United States as a country was reaching maturity, and growing fast. At the end of Monroe's period in office, the original thirteen States had grown to twenty-four.

With Monroe the rule of the Virginia gentlemen died, but it died with a flourish. When Monroe had been re-elected for his second term, only one vote in the Electoral College was cast against him, for the stated reason that history should not record any man as being unanimously re-elected to this office except George Washington. But all of the prestige of long tenure in the White House could not save that dynasty from eclipse, and the Presidency was passed to John Quincy Adams as a stop-gap in the face of the onrushing western horde.

Adams lasted four years, in some ways less successful a President than he had been a diplomat and Cabinet adviser. Then like his father, John Quincy, also a conservative, was swept aside after one term by the wave of new ideas clamoring at the White House doors.

The loudest voice in the new era was that of Henry Clay, but he had a potent rival in the less eloquent but more blunt Andrew Jackson, and Jackson, too, was a war hero. When the new era swooped to a peaceful resolution in the White House, Jackson was the choice.

Mirrored centerpiece purchased in France by Monroe for the State Dining Room

French clock with figurine of Hannibal

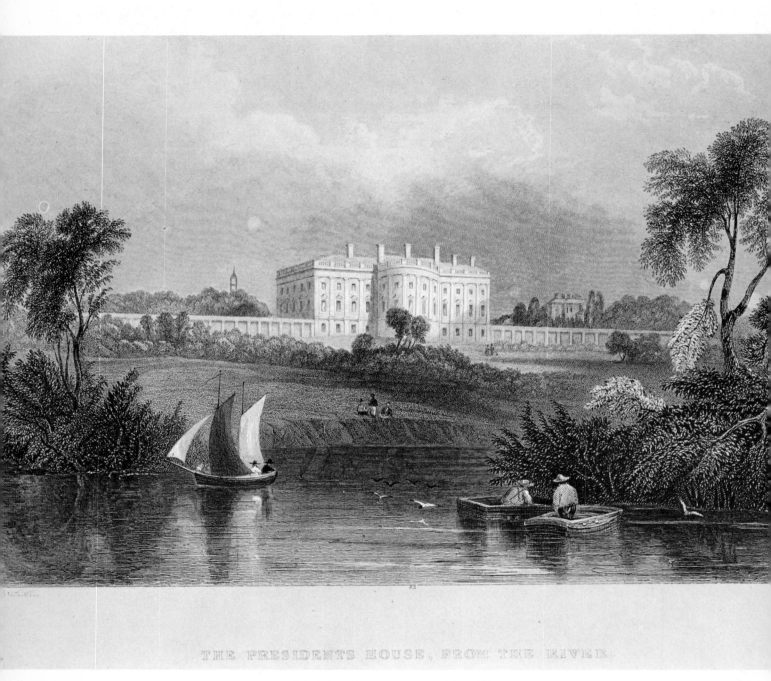

THE PRESIDENTS HOUSE, FROM THE RIVER.

The White House romanticized, late 1830s

Andrew Jackson's Inaugural, on March 4, 1829, was a revolution in every manner except for its peaceful development. It affected almost every detail of the position of the President, the social customs of the White House, the nature of the power of the office, and the President's relationship to the public. Knee breeches and powdered wigs for dress occasions disappeared from the official scene. More importantly, the new President took his mandate from the people and no longer from the coteries of State leaders who themselves were mainly the entrenched "names" of the dominant older communities.

Even the Vice President, the courtly and oratorical John C. Calhoun, was a self-made man and professional politician rather than the scion of an "aristocratic" family, although his wife and distant cousin, dark and sultry Floride Calhoun, brought to their marriage the money he needed to support his career.

All of the change took place in what had been established as the traditional manner, with the oath of office administered to the tall, taciturn new President by the aging John Marshall, Chief Justice of the United States. The oath was administered on the east portico of the Capitol, and ironically John Quincy Adams followed his father's bitter "tradition" by declining to attend the swearing-in of his successor.

Nevertheless, these outward forms, while attesting to orderly change, were deceptive. A great deal more was happening than a mere continuation of old ceremony. Both liberals and conservatives recognized the change and liked or dreaded it, according to their own feelings.

In Daniel Webster's conservative viewpoint, the people who gathered for the Inaugural were a "monstrous crowd" of new-type Americans, many garbed in the frontier clothes of buckskin and coonskin hats. Another diarist wrote of the crowd as an "expectant host, a sort of Praetorian band, which, having borne in upon their shields their idolized leader, claimed the rewards of the hard-fought contest." Yet Francis Scott Key, who fifteen years earlier had written "The Star-Spangled Banner," and now was a prosperous lawyer, still could see the day of Jackson's Inaugural as "beautiful" and "sublime."

The new tenant of the White House was a man who, in a different political climate, might have seized leadership without striving for a normal election. He was the firebrand that most Americans seemed to want in order to break the self-hypnotism caused by the quiet grandeur in which the country had become immersed.

Jackson was not a young Lochinvar in shining armor. When he was elected he was sixty-one years old—venerable for his day. In his body he carried more than one lead slug from duels, and the reputation of at least one killing of a slanderer of his wife. In his youth he had been a

Senator, had tried for and lost a Presidential election four years earlier, had been orphaned in his teens, had settled as a lawyer in the frontier country when Nashville, Tennessee, was a stockaded settlement, and in the War of 1812 had beaten an Indian army and a crack British one. No predecessor in the White House had even imagined, let alone experienced, such a life; nor had any of their intimate friends.

Jackson's entrance into Washington indeed had the appearance of a conqueror's celebration; he had progressed up the Cumberland and Ohio Rivers by barge and thence overland to Washington by coach, with one triumphant reception after another. Every stop had been marked by salutes of cannons and oratory. Perhaps some of this was arranged by the skillful Major W. B. Lewis, who had been his campaign manager. Whatever the cause, the effect was awe-inspiring.

Yet this backwoodsman—as his critics termed Jackson—acted at least as royally as the Indian chiefs he had subjugated. First among the Presidents to do so, he included in his party an "official portraitist," R. E. W. Earl, who would spend the next eight years doing only pictures of Jackson. And he took with him a personal entourage, quite separate from Cabinet members, headed by F. P. Blair, the editor, who founded *The Globe,* a newspaper for Jacksonian publicity.

In his choice of close political subordinates, Jackson also acted without much regard for public opinion. His Secretary of State was Martin Van Buren, the New York political leader sometimes sarcastically called "the little Duke of Kinderhook," and his Secretary of War was J. H. Eaton, who attended Jackson's Inaugural with his bride, the former Peg O'Neale, whom he had met while stopping at the tavern Indian Queen, owned by her father. Jackson named his nephew, Andrew Jackson Donelson, as private secretary, and his daughter-in-law, Mrs. Donelson, as hostess-designate. A brood of Donelson children gave a lively touch to the White House.

To cap the total irony of this changing of the guard in the Presidency on Inaugural Day, the White House was nearly wrecked by the "reception" held by the new frontier President. His followers had come to celebrate the induction of "their" President from as far as New Orleans and from points in the northern wilderness. Refreshments for twenty thousand persons were prepared in the White House, together with a monster cheese sent by an anonymous old soldier.

The refreshments ran out, the visitors reportedly did almost as much damage to the furnishings, except for fire, as the British had in 1814, and Jackson eventually had to "escape" from his own gala by climbing out of a window and fleeing for the night to a room in Gadsby's Tavern, in Alexandria.

To the older Washington crowd, now the "outsiders," the most ominous threat to their establishment was the forthright statement by the new President, "To the Victor Belong the Spoils."

So much has been made of Jackson's ruthless political leadership and the imprint he left on the new Democratic Party that his personal imprint on the White House is seldom remembered, except for the O'Neale affair, in which he suffered his only defeat. It might have been different had Mrs. Jackson lived to enter the White House, but she did not, and about all that is remembered about her is that she smoked a pipe.

By this time, Washington had begun to develop social traditions that were deadly serious to the players in the political waltz. The Diplomatic Corps had expanded, wealthy families had begun to open houses there for the social season. They looked upon Jackson as the frontiersman, exclusive of his other sides; it is unlikely that any had even seen his private estate, the Hermitage.

He was compared disparagingly with the elegant Britsh Minister, Sir Charles Vaughan, whose annual ball in 1829 brought the carriages of four hundred "leading families" to his door. Baron Krudener, the Russian Minister, was Vaughan's social rival. Mrs. Samuel Smith, no longer the dewy-eyed bride of Jefferson's protegé but now a writer and arbiter of the social scene, could entertain more than one hundred and twenty persons at supper dances at Sydney; but Mrs. Porter, wife of the Commodore, was the most lavish hostess among non-diplomats, with a band for dancing at her receptions on alternate Mondays. Persico, an Italian sculptor, settled in Washington for a career of translating the beauties of the day into marble busts. Who needed paved streets or sewers in such an elegant atmosphere?

But in this atmosphere Jackson found himself immediately involved in a situation with Peg O'Neale. He chose to make an issue of it.

Four years before Jackson's Inaugural he had visited Washington with Mrs. Jackson and experienced his defeat in his first try for the Presidency. At the Indian Queen, Peg helped her father serve the distinguished guests, including Senator Eaton, and Mrs. Jackson reportedly became fond of the girl.

The only rub was that Peg O'Neale had once been married, and that her husband, a sailor, had committed suicide over her promiscuous activities in his absences. Senator Eaton was also said by gossips to have enjoyed certain premarital favors. In the social mores of the day, his only indiscretion was in marrying her.

Jackson actually passed the word that he expected Mrs. Eaton to be treated exactly as other wives in his official family, but Mrs. Smith boiled up in leadership of the opposition:

"As for the *new lady* [the italics are hers]," she wrote, "public opinion ever just and impartial seems to have triumphed over personal feelings and intrigues and finally doomed her to continue in her pristine lowly condition. A stand, a *noble* stand, I may say, since it is a stand taken against power and favoritism, has been made by the ladies of Washington, and not even the President's wishes, in favor of his dearest personal friend, can influence them to violate the respect due to virtue, by visiting one who has left her strait and narrow path.

"With the exception of two or three rather insignificant personages, who trembled for their husbands' offices, not a lady has visited her, and so far from being inducted into the President's house, she is, I am told, scarcely mentioned by the females of his family."

Actually Martin Van Buren, from his lofty perch as Secretary of State, did stand by Mrs. Eaton, but then he was a bachelor. The losing fight continued a long while, even echoing two years later, in 1831, when Jackson reportedly forced the recall of Meinherr Huggens, the Dutch Minister, because Madame Huggens refused to receive Mrs. Eaton.

None of this episode, of course, enhanced admiration for Jackson in the tight little society established in the swamps bordering the Potomac. Such gossip also accentuated other tales that the President spent his private evenings in slippers and without a coat, reading, while his grandchildren scampered around him. And much was made of the fact that Jackson's new list of furnishings for the East Room included twenty spittoons. The number was apparently the important factor, because every house had spittoons in this snuff-taking and tobacco-chewing age. Perhaps the gossips gave less credit than Jackson deserved for his devotion to the White House, which was not even second to that of Jefferson.

For it was Jackson who had the imagination and first mustered the means to complete the White House, fortunately just before the dead hand of nineteenth-century ugliness captured architectural fancy. He worked with Van Buren, who seemed to have had a flair for design, and who supervised the first fencing in of part of the White House grounds.

Due to Jackson's interest, Hoban was able to complete the more than forty-year project of building and rebuilding the White House. First, the aging architect completed the East Room with paneling and ornamental beams, following the original design. The porticoes, as seen today, were added at last from plans originally suggested by Dr. William Thornton but heartily approved by the architect of the White House.

Graceful wings, a single story in height, were extended east and west of the main building as architecturally integrated housing for the carriages, stables, and other "offices." And perhaps the most up-to-date of all innovations was the laying of iron pipes for a clean supply of fresh water to the house in place of wooden troughs from nearby springs formerly in use.

In the meantime the White House furnishings, which were then almost ruined by the crowds that tramped through the rooms, were renewed by Jackson, and he obtained a new French dinner service and crystal that included nine sizes of wine glasses.

Also, the first formal gardening was done around the White House by a young man who became internationally famous for his designs and books describing them, in a lifetime that extended only thirty-seven years. His name was Andrew Jackson Downing, a name which suggests nepotism was involved, but he was a New Yorker born in the crop of 1815 babies, when a good tithe of all baby boys were being named in honor of the victor of the Battle of New Orleans.

When occasion dictated, Jackson could be the gracious and interested host to a wide variety of guests, aside from his political cronies who normally fill the pages of his biographies. For instance, there was the visit to Washington of Miss Harriet Martineau, the distinguished and brilliant British sociologist, who was touring America and who was invited to Washington under the sponsorship of Mrs. Smith. This visit was in 1835, after six years of Jackson's "reign," when Henry Clay had returned to Washington as a Senator, and when Robert R. Livingston, the notable of New York, had joined Jackson's Cabinet.

The British Minister took his distinguished countrywoman to call on the President, and Jackson promptly arranged a dinner in her honor. Mrs. Smith reported that she was embarrassed at having one Washington hostess ask Miss Martineau what novels she had written. But no such contretemps arose at the White House dinner. There, while she sat and listened to conversation with the aid of the new-fashioned ear trumpet, statesmen discussed her works on political economy.

As for White House dinners, no menus remain from the period, but the Martineau visit gave Mrs. Smith a reason to describe eating habits. The gossipy reporter noted that Mrs. Levi Woodbury served eighteen guests a total of thirty meat courses, and then gave some details of her own "simple" dinner for twelve persons, served as was then customary at 5 P.M.

The Smith dinner began with a fish chowder, served alongside a boned fish. It was followed by canvasback duck and pheasants. Then came ham and turkey, garnished with partridges, mutton chops, and sweetbreads. The side dishes were macaroni and oyster pie, with celery, spinach, salsify, and cauliflower. The dinner was rounded off with ice cream and a pyramid of fruit, served on a large tray around whose sides were clustered blancmange, cakes, custards, and sweetmeats. Mrs. Smith also noted that at such formal dinners guests were not served the unfashionable and common vegetables— potatoes and beets—or the undistinguished puddings and pies.

After such dinners, the women gossiped in one room and the men drank in another. Unless the guests were going on to a dance or supper party elsewhere, the dinner hostess would provide a "light supper" and tea about nine o'clock.

Eventually Jackson's entertainments and the other expenses of his office caught up with him, as has been the case with many other Presidents.

He was a meticulous bookkeeper, and personally kept his own accounts of official expenditures and of what he considered his private ones while in the Presidency. When his term ended he owed $6,000, which he could not pay from cash in hand. Accordingly he mortgaged in advance the cotton crop anticipated from the Hermitage to raise this money.

The irony of this debt was due somewhat to Jackson's lofty attitude toward gifts to the President. While Jackson was settling his Washington affairs, a gift arrived from the Sultan of Morocco, a fine lion. Jackson gave it to the local orphans home, which immediately sold it for $3,350.

In the year that Jackson packed to move from the White House, the building got a new neighbor and an old legend returning to the scene when the widowed Dolley Madison left Montpelier and the memories of her husband behind her. She purchased a small but comfortable house on the street north of the White House, and just opposite the eastern corner of its grounds. She was no longer wealthy, largely due to the costs of Madison's long retirement and the demands reportedly made on her by her extravagant son, Payne Todd. And she was careless with money.

Perhaps a typical mature lady of sixty-nine years would have gotten along very well on the remainder of her fortune, but Dolley Madison was hardly typical. She persistently dyed her curls that bobbed under her turbans a raven black, was one of the first to learn and then to teach the younger set the new waltz dance, and entertained her friends at intimate dinners where Daniel Webster usually was the center of conversation. She went out as much as any younger woman. And in time finally Mrs. Polk, usually identified as stiff-necked and prim because she espoused prohibition, provided a special seat for Dolley at a White House reception while the younger wife of a President stood to receive her guests.

Furthermore, Dolley's friends were not just the rich and the famous; they included former servants as well. Jean Pierre Sioussat had worked his way from former chef to clerkship in a bank. He took on the volunteer chore of keeping false accounts on Dolley's household expenditures, to conceal her poverty from her. An aged Negro, Paul Jennings, who had been Madison's personal servant until he could purchase his freedom, was now Daniel Webster's valet. Finally Dolley discovered that much of the food served on her table was being brought directly from Webster's kitchen to hers, with the Senator's connivance.

Finally Dolley's plight took on much the proportions of a project to preserve a national monument, going entirely beyond the bounds of politics. Amos Lawrence, of Massachusetts, sent her a present of a dress made from silk produced in one of his mills. Robert C. Winthrop, of Massachusetts, offered to raise a fund to provide an annuity, but this Dolley declined.

In 1848, the last year of Dolley's life, she announced that she would hold a "raffle" of some of her effects, which in turn brought a wave of protest, and caused Webster and his fellow Senator, James Buchanan, to hatch a special scheme.

They knew that in the attic of Dolley's house was a locked leather trunk that contained Madison's last prized collection of papers. In the wave of friendly sentiment for the old lady, Congress passed an appropriation of $25,000 to purchase the papers, on her eightieth birthday in 1848.

Why $25,000? The sponsors knew her needs. They placed $20,000 in a trust fund to guarantee her future, used $3,000 to pay off a mortgage held by John Jacob Astor, and, among other items, redeemed a silver service pawned for $70 and a gold chain pledged for $20.

Perhaps Dolley Madison has grown larger than she was in life. During her life span in Washington—before, during, and after the White House period—she possessed much more charm than the other White House mistresses. None after Jackson among the Presidents, until Lincoln, could compare with her husband.

The White House at last reached a point which showed that democracies, like royal dynasties, however much they glitter in public show, sometimes fade away from greatness.

The "fading" started with Martin Van Buren and continued on to 1861, when Lincoln entered the mansion as the sad leader in a troubled time. And yet outwardly the completed White House left

by Jackson continued to become more magnificent.

After Van Buren came William Henry Harrison, John Tyler, James K. Polk, Zachary Taylor, Millard Fillmore, Franklin Pierce, and James Buchanan. With them Washington achieved more paved streets, a few sewers, and a water system. In their tenures the White House occasionally sparkled socially. Due to world

White House during John Tyler's Administration

A Presidential reception in the East Room

Death of Zachary Taylor at the White House in 1850

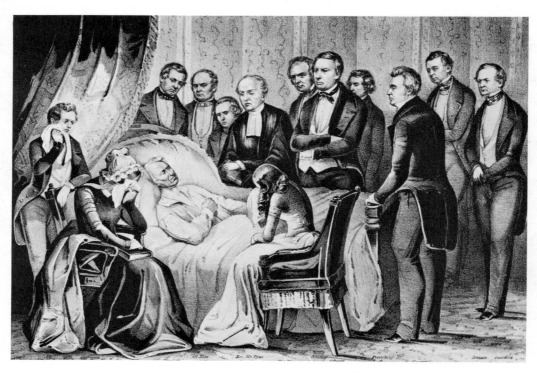

politics, in a revolutionary era, the Diplomatic Corps became larger and more colorful in its assemblage of distinguished foreign titles.

But for the time the bloom was off the rose, first glowing with the personalities of the great classic leaders and afterward leavened with the new democracy that was typified by Andrew Jackson. Oratory took, in many cases, the place of statesmanship; glamour the place of brains. Also, the artificial style of flattery became so pronounced that one continually asks, "Was the beauty really so beautiful?" or "Were the beaux as gallant as described?" These descriptions seem to vary in direct ratio to the fortunes behind the names or the context of the occasions.

Van Buren, in his single term, was a prime example of the ups and downs of political popularity as reflected in the White House. Van Buren was welcomed into office with an Inaugural Ball at Carusi's, cheered through the streets and tendered the tribute of a massed call by the Diplomatic Corps in full dress uniforms. But immediately after being installed in office, perhaps resentful of his beginning as son of an innkeeper, he overspent appropriations for the new White House furnishings, including the purchase of gold spoons, and closed the White House doors to the public except on New Year's Day—an order quickly rescinded. Long a widower, he had at his dinner table four sons, of whom the eldest was Martin Van Buren, Jr.

Congressional leaders already resented him, nicknamed the little man with his big airs "Martin the First." Their resentment grew into apprehension when a depression began in the middle of his single term. Then the hailstones of criticism rained down on his household when his eldest son married Angelica Singleton, who, as White House hostess, reinstated the raised platform introduced by Elizabeth Monroe. She received at receptions with a headdress bearing the three feathers denoting presentation at the Court of St. James's.

None of this was really important, but circumstances made it so. People conveniently overlooked the fact that Angelica met the Van Burens while she was visiting Dolley Madison, and that she was intimate with Queen Victoria's court as a relative of Andrew Stevenson, the American Minister there. Furthermore, the junior Mrs. Van Buren had guests announced as in the olden days, and this seemed to modern democrats a trifle upstage.

On the night before William Henry Harrison was to have his own Inaugural Day, crowds marched up and down before the White House chanting, "Van, Van is a used-up man."

General Harrison had been elected after another experiment in running a war hero for the Presidency. His candidacy had been fortified with Tyler as his running mate, but without the least expectation that Tyler would sit in the White House. Harrison was President for only one month, from March 4 to April 4, which time he spent in bed with a fatal illness that began with a chill when he rode horseback in a cold rain in his own Inaugural Parade . . . and Tyler was the new President.

In the succession of mediocrities prior

Mrs. James K. Polk, the stern Calvinist

to 1861, the master of the White House was generally elected on the basis of being a "safe" man, an individual with no outstanding strong points—a non-leader. For its time, the system had a certain partial merit. Any historical summary notes that in this era Texas was added to the Union, and a little later California, that the northwest frontier with Canada was clarified without a war; that canals and railroads tied together the rivers of commerce, and that American scientific genius produced the telegraph. Maybe it was better, from that standpoint, for the White House to be more of a ceremonial place than the heart of Government.

But history also was preparing to exact a terrible price for this role of compromise and overlooking of problems. The strong men and the strong voices passed from the White House to the Congress— the voices of contention and division, particularly from the South which saw in the rising West and the industrially prosperous North the loss of what had once been its private domain.

In effect, the Presidency was a power symbol representing two irreconcilable older American cultures, the Northern industrial and the Southern agricultural. The new West might well have tilted the alliance toward the South, for it too was mainly agricultural, but every new State created in the West was a free State, so these sided politically with the free North.

Americans and foreigners never could quite understand why Washington, D. C., as the capital of a free country, teemed with slaves. Few remained in private houses, but they were the cheap labor of the city—not just imported but actually bought and sold on the auction block. All that the law required was that a clear title be held by the owner.

The fiery arguments of the Abolitionists rumbled in the North and many Southerners progressively freed their slaves, but at the heart of the argument was property, and property rights were king. So the White House as an institution walked a slippery path of compromise and division, trying to forget old Andrew Jackson's exclamation years before, "The Union! It must be preserved!"

In 1842 a meeting in Washington between America's most prominent author and Charles Dickens served to leave a record of Washington and the White House that is picturesque and relatively free of the nauseous clichés of the contemporary gossip writers.

Dickens was in the United States to lecture, and to write about the country for his British audience. In the course of Dickens' visit, Washington Irving was invited to the White House to receive a commission as the new Minister to Spain and to attend a reception in his honor. Irving invited Dickens to be present.

Dickens was living at Fuller's Hotel, situated at Pennsylvania Avenue and Fourteenth Street. From Dickens' report, allowing for his own prejudices against America in general—except for the munificent lecture fees—come these observations:

The hotel in which we live is a long row of small houses fronting on the street, and opening on the back upon a common yard, in which hangs a great triangle. Whenever a servant is wanted, somebody beats the triangle from one stroke to seven, according to the number of the house in which his presence is required and as all the servants are always being wanted, and none of them ever come, this enlivening regime is in full performance the whole day.

Clothes are drying in the same yard; female slaves with cotton handkerchiefs twisted around their heads, are running to and fro on the hotel business; black waiters cross and recross with dishes in their hands; two great dogs are playing upon a mound of loose bricks in the center of the little square; a pig is turning his stomach up to the sun, and grunting, "That's comfortable," and neither the men nor the women, nor the dogs nor the pig, nor any created creature takes the smallest notice of the triangle, which is tinkling madly all the time. . . .

I walk to the window, and look across the road upon a long straggling row of houses, one

Rural visitors in the East Room

story high, terminating nearly opposite, but a little to the left, in a little piece of waste ground with frowzy grass, which looks like a small piece of country that had taken to drinking, and quite lost itself. Standing anyhow and all wrong, upon this open space, like something meteoric that had fallen down from the moon, is an odd, lop-sided kind of wooden building, that looks like a church, with a flag staff as long as itself sticking out of a steeple something larger than a tea-chest. Under the window a large stand of coaches, whose slave drivers are sunning themselves upon the steps of our door, and talking idly together.

It is sometimes called the City of Magnificent Distances, but it might be with great propriety the City of Magnificent Intention, for it is only in taking a bird's-eye view of it from the top of the Capitol that one can at all comprehend the vast design of its projector, an 77 aspiring Frenchman. Spacious avenues that begin in nothing and lead nowhere, streets miles long that only want houses, roads and inhabitants; public buildings that need but a public to complete; and ornaments of great thoroughfares, which only lack thoroughfares to ornaments—are its leading features. One might fancy the season was over and most of the houses gone out of town forever with their masters. To the admirers of the cities it is a Barmecide feast; a pleasant field for the imagination to roam in; a monument raised to a deceased project, with not even a legible inscription to record its departed greatness.

Such as it is, it is likely to remain. It was originally chosen for the seat of government, as a means of averting jealousies and interests in the different States; and very probably, too, as being remote from mobs, a consideration not to be slighted even in America.

It has no trade or commerce of its own, having little of population beyond the President and his establishment, the members of the legislature who reside here during the session, the government clerks and officers employed in the various departments, the keepers of the hotels and boarding houses, and the tradesmen who supply their tables. It is very unhealthy. Few people would live in Washington, I take it, who are not obliged to reside there.

These were impressions on a hot and sunny afternoon, so often echoed by other visitors. Yet as if in an effort to redeem the worst impressions, the party in honor of Irving gave Dickens another viewpoint, which was recorded in an equally honest and interesting fashion:

I went with my wife, at about 10. There was a pretty dense crowd of carriages and people in the courtyard and so far as I could make out there were no very clear regulations for the taking up and setting down of company.

There were certainly no policemen to soothe startled horses, either by swinging at their bridles or flourishing truncheons in their eyes; and I am ready to make oath that no inoffensive persons were knocked violently on the head, or poked acutely in the backs or stomachs, or brought to a standstill by any such harsh means, and then taken into custody for not moving on.

Our carriage reached the porch in its turn, without any blustering, swearing, shouting or other disturbances and we dismounted with as much ease and comfort as though we had been escorted by the whole metropolitan force from A to Z inclusive.

White House during James Buchanan's Administration

The suite of rooms on the ground floor was lighted up and a military band was playing in the hall. In the smaller drawing room, the centre of a circle of company, were the President and his daughter-in-law, who acted as the lady of the Mansion; and a very interesting, graceful and accomplished lady, too. One gentleman who stood among this group appeared to take upon himself the functions of a master of ceremonies. I saw no other officers or attendants, and none was needed.

The great drawing room, which I have already mentioned, and the other chambers in the ground floor were crowded to excess. The company was not in our sense of the term select, for it comprehended persons of very many grades and classes; nor was there any great display of costly attire.

That these visitors, too, whatever their station, were not without some refinement of taste and appreciation of intellectual gifts and gratitude to those men who, by the powerful exercise of their abilities, shed new charms and appreciation upon the home of their countrymen, and elevate their character in other lands, was most earnestly testified by their reception to Washington Irving, my dear friend, who had recently been appointed Minister to the Court of Spain, and who was among them that night, in his new character, for the first and last time before going abroad. . . .

Dickens might well have written his description in any year up to 1860. Only minor details would have changed; in the White House there was only a change in mediocre personalities. A few highlights of personal interest alone broke the routine. One of these involved Tyler, who in 1844 was fifty-four years of age, and had been widowed for two years. He was the first President to marry while in office.

The Navy Yard had installed on the brig *Princeton* a new, large cannon named the "Peace Maker," and a party of three hundred persons headed by the President were invited to see its initial firing. In the party were members of the Cabinet and other ranking officials including Senator David Gardiner, of New York, who was accompanied by his twenty-year-old daughter. When the cannon was prepared for firing, President Tyler decided to remain in a lounge below deck, where he was visiting with Miss Gardiner.

The gun exploded, killing a number of

White House during the Polk Administration

spectators including Senator Gardiner, Secretary of State Abel P. Upshar, Secretary of the Navy Thomas W. Gilmer, and Commodore Beverly Kenyon, as well as severely wounding Secretary of War William Wilkins. This was the worst tragedy, in numbers of political leaders killed, in the country's history. Three months later President Tyler went as quietly as a President could to New York, where he married Miss Gardiner.

Tyler did not run for re-election, but threw his support to Polk, a Tennessean. Mrs. Polk gave a bland and puzzling touch to the White House that was ascribed to her fanatical religious tendencies as she grew older. This also led to other gossip that had not touched earlier Presidents, to the effect that old Andrew Jackson had "arranged" Polk's marriage in order to prevent possible scandal or a fatal duel that threatened the career of his protegé if he did not settle down. If so, Mrs. Polk was a settler both socially and in her assumption of the job of secretary to her husband. She served dinners without wine or liquor, and banned cards, dancing, and all other types of entertainment in the White House.

When Polk left office, General Zachary Taylor took to the establishment a frontier wife, who ran the housekeeping and did her own sewing in an upper room where she could smoke her pipe in peaceful privacy, leaving the duties of hostess to a twenty-two-year-old daughter.

Gas was piped into the mansion in Polk's Administration. Taylor's successor, Millard Fillmore, introduced central heating and plumbing of the newer sort. It became a matter of Washington gossip that Fillmore bathed both regularly and elegantly, commented upon in terms indicating how unusual this habit was. And the gossip was so precise that he was known to use Corinthian Oil of Cream and concentrated extract of eglantine.

But there was more to Fillmore's regime than his advocacy of bathing. President Fillmore represented the new political prototype of the truly self-made man —his only tutor being his wife. Mrs. Fillmore had been a schoolteacher—Miss Abigail Powers—in Cayuga County, New York, when she and Fillmore were married. President Fillmore was virtually uneducated, but in four years plodded through a course of studies laid out by his wife.

When the Fillmores entered the White House, the President's wife noted with dismay that there was not a book in the mansion. At her urging, the Congress appropriated money for the first White House library. She purchased sets of Dickens and Thackeray, several histories, and other works that suggested she may have duplicated the reading laid out years earlier for her bridegroom.

Under the chandeliers in the East Room passed a wide variety of celebrities typical of the times: General Louis Kossuth, the Hungarian patriot; William M. Tweed, who would become the most notorious Boss of Tammany Hall; and on another visit, Washington Irving, who introduced another special guest, William Makepeace Thackeray.

In Fillmore's name, too, history was made, first in 1851, when the United States sent a thousand tons of exhibits to the first foreign exposition it ever entered, at the Crystal Palace in London. And a year later Commodore Perry led the naval-diplomatic mission to pry open the doors of Japan.

When James Buchanan was inaugurated on March 4, 1857, he began a single term that would supply a plot for as fantastic an opera as has ever been written. In elegance and glamour—plus beauty—here was perhaps the unsurpassed Administration of the nineteenth century, playing out its role in a last bright dawn before the Civil War.

Officially Buchanan did his best to act as a mediator in the rising political conflict, only to see his term end with seven States in secession and another "President" sitting in Richmond, Virginia.

If superlatives in the descriptions of the day may be trusted, Buchanan's Inaugural Reception was the largest yet. It was followed by a ball and banquet in a temporary building 220 feet long that was erected in Judiciary Square.

For a day at least it seemed that Washington believed that the war clouds could be dissipated, and that the fears about the future could be allayed, by paying this tribute to a new President, already distinguished as a former Secretary of State and Minister to England. In its celebration the crowd feasted on 400 gallons of oysters, 500 quarts of chicken salad, 1,200 quarts of ice cream, 500 quarts of jellies, 60 saddles of mutton and four of venison, eight rounds of beef and 75 hams, among other items.

The oath of office had been administered that day by Roger Brooke Taney, Chief Justice of the United States, who was already preparing a Supreme Court decision to be announced only two days later. This so-called Dred Scott decision upheld the right to possess slaves in free territory and tore apart the Missouri Compromise. No single act contributed more, at least emotionally, to the fires of anger against the South kindled in the North by the Abolitionists.

Outwardly Buchanan played the role of compromiser, seemingly attempting by courtly gestures to maintain an appearance of unity in the Federal Government. As his hostess he introduced his niece and adopted daughter, Harriet Lane, whose portraits surely do not do justice to her beautiful figure and face. Around her Buchanan built a background of elegance: he established new rules on protocol and built a hothouse for roses and grapes off the west terrace.

Surprisingly, from reports of the period, the public seemed to approve all this, including the elegance displayed by Buchanan in his carriages, his clothes, and the White House services. Perhaps life in the mansion had become for the moment a symbolic antidote for political fears.

In a period so recently noted for resentment of European fashions, Buchanan even weathered criticism and won compliments for entertaining the highest-ranking representative from the British crown yet to visit the United States.

There was a little of the element of comic opera in this visit, in a day when royalty could pretend to be not quite royal, by traveling incognito. On October 3, 1860, there arrived in Washington a diplomat called Baron Renfrew, who was in actuality the disguised son of Queen

Victoria, Prince of Wales and future Edward VII of Great Britain. He was concluding a tour of the eastern parts of Canada and the United States. This disguise presumably eliminated embarrassment that might arise in official circumstances either for bruises to democratic sentiment or recollections of recent wars.

But Buchanan was not fooled by the disguised name. He not only gave the simple baron a banquet and reception, but also vacated his own bedroom to house his guest.

One month after the baron departed, and before his mother could send off a personal note thanking Buchanan and Miss Lane for their hospitality to her disguised son, Lincoln was elected President.

Before Buchanan went out of office he presided over an elegant White House that had sunk to one of the low points of prestige in history. Half a dozen attempts were made by others to uphold his hand, but these efforts only emphasized the weakness. Also, as a "lame duck" President no one would have taken seriously his actions had he made inspired gestures.

Lincoln's election was interpreted by the States generally as meaning that the raw-boned, graceless President-elect was bringing into office a policy to preserve the Union at any price. In his long absence from Washington, awaiting his own Inaugural, it was Lincoln's unseen political presence that actually vitiated the authority of the White House, leaving in the vacuum the opportunities for turmoil that now seem unthinkable.

The debates in Congress were dominated by the question of secession. Emotions had become so strained that a group of Congressional leaders, assuming authority the President should have demanded, invited Tyler to come back and head an informal Committee of Public Safety to forestall rioting in the Capital city. General Winfield Scott, of Mexican War fame, was called from New York to plan an armed defense for the city. Early in January the government of Virginia invited to other Southern States to meet in Richmond and plan a course of action. Jefferson Davis, former Secretary of War and now a leading Senator from Mississippi, resigned to serve the forthcoming Confederacy. South Carolina already had seceded from the Union. On February 1, Virginia and five other Southern States joined North Carolina in this move, and voted to establish a capital at Montgomery, Alabama.

Buchanan accompanied Lincoln to the Capitol for the Inaugural ceremonies, and the new President rode back to the White House in a carriage surrounded so densely by a cavalry "honor guard" that hardly any spectators saw him.

From 1861 to 1865 the White House grew in prestige and power, stumblingly and haltingly at first, after a rapid dimming of the social glitter. As in all Administrations before and after Lincoln, the mansion reflected the opportunities, the challenges, and the strengths and weaknesses of its occupants.

For the first few weeks after Lincoln's Inaugural, despite the acts of secession by the Southern States, while Lincoln felt his way carefully, it seemed that politics would be conducted outside the White House walls. Of course, this would be only symbolic, since the President's own office, those of his secretaries, and his Cabinet rooms all were on the second floor of the mansion. The Cabinet members themselves had their own office buildings, but the White House was as yet the President's home at night, his office in the daytime, and generally a building open to the curious public.

To celebrate the political victory there was the traditional and huge Inaugural Ball, arranged long in advance by the men who shared Lincoln's victory. To celebrate her own social triumph, Mary Todd Lincoln laid out a program of receptions and dinners that promised to set some new kind of social record. Three large receptions, for which serving was done by a New York caterer, were held in four weeks. But then there fell a sudden social lull, indicating that perhaps the slow-to-arouse Lincoln had sat down and had a serious talk with his charming but ambitious wife.

Probably the first photograph taken of the White House, by Brady, around 1860

An artist's conception of a White House reception in March, 1865. Shown in the drawing are President Lincoln, Mrs. Lincoln, General and Mrs. Grant, General Sherman, and Secretary of War Stanton.

By mid-April the big receptions were canceled. Mrs. Lincoln received ladies only on Tuesday nights. The President reserved Saturday afternoons for meeting social callers and it was decreed that only one great reception would be held each year, on New Year's Day.

In his day-long and frequently night-long conferences, Lincoln had first to use the White House as a school in which to learn his new political responsibilities, and then to execute decisions in matters

where he had relatively little skilled help. The Congress on longer contained an elite of giants of the caliber of Webster, Clay, and Calhoun—all imaginative men despite their other differences. Whole blocs of seats in the Senate and House were vacated by the departure of Southern members. Much of the skilled military branch were going or had gone, reflecting the relatively large proportion of Southerners who favored military service as a career.

Typical of the last group was Robert E.

Sketch of Lincoln and a California hunter

Lee, colonel in the Army, former Superintendent of West Point and the officer sent in 1859 to put down John Brown's revolt at Harper's Ferry. At this point Lee was a respected officer for whom promotion had been blocked by the decades of peace. But as Lincoln's plans proceeded, it was evident that a successor must be appointed for the aged General Scott, still titular Commander-in-Chief.

Early in February, Montgomery Blair, Postmaster General and son of the Jack-

sonian editor, invited Lee to his house for a private dinner. The unconfirmed but accepted story is that Lincoln also sat at the dinner table. Blair had a delicate assignment, entirely out of line for a Postmaster General, but he was a unique man in politics, as had been his father. The task Lincoln had given him had to be handled outside of official lines, or rumors would have been telegraphed across the country before morning.

In the course of the evening, Lee was 85

offered command of the United States Army, as well as many compliments about his military record and the strong sentiments he had expressed and shown in loyalty to his country.

Lee gave a reply that may have been anticipated, but could not have been elicited without an inquiry. He appreciated the offer, but he could not and would not fight or direct fighting against his native Virginia. He rode from Blair House across the river to his palatial estate at Arlington, never to return. The official record shows that Lee declined the offer of command on April 18, 1861, resigned his commission on April 20, and on April 23 accepted command of the forces being raised by Virginia.

The loss of Lee was one of the greatest tragedies faced by Lincoln in the early days of his White House trials. The orators and the firebrands could shout and rave, but in his quiet manner, his courtli-

ness and high skills, Lee would have been both military leader and symbol.

Nothing epitomized more the loneliness and the heavy responsibilities of the White House. There had been wars before, but these wars had been far-flung, even though one swept over Washington in its climactic finish. Yet these wars, too, had been against foreign powers, with the American Government solidly aligned behind the figure of the Presidency.

In this war the President was alone. He was firmly enough backed by sentiment in the North, well supported by the volunteers who answered the call to join his army, but he shouldered almost in a vacuum the awful responsibilities that were detailed so eloquently in the words of the Constitution. No one else could share responsibility for the selection of a succession of generals, each the best possible choice at the time but none as good as Lee—until Grant (the heroically named

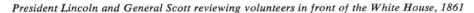

President Lincoln and General Scott reviewing volunteers in front of the White House, 1861

Ulysses S. Grant) finally appeared as a volunteer and re-established himself.

The politicians in the Cabinet, the leaders in Congress, could do material things such as preparing the incomplete Treasury Building as a last redoubt in case of invasion of Washington, fortifying the Capitol against the same possibility, quartering of troops in the Capitol as a massive staging and training area, building of barracks to shelter the hordes of slaves who now fled to freedom from the South. As a political leader Lincoln could confer on these projects, approve them as Commander-in-Chief, and in the name of the Government approve the sometimes almost criminal war contracts made by the profiteers.

But as a human being, he carried the burden of the Presidency on his stooped and narrow shoulders alone, and in doing so he made the White House the great and shining thing that it gradually became —by his humanity rather than his genius. The worse the war went, the simpler and more dignified and more patient became the White House leadership.

Lincoln rode to the Capitol to visit the troops quartered there. He went out to inspect the defenses of the Capital city. Wrapped in a blanket he spent long nights, with no guard or other show of office, seated beside the lone telegrapher in the War Department Building.

The first year of his leadership was the hardest—a year of defeats and no victories, of great suggestions and plans but no real means to put them into effect, of watching the fantastic achievements of the Confederates as Lee and T. J. (Stone-

wall) Jackson outmaneuvered the best of the Union generals.

This was the year of patient effort to restore the Union to what it had been before the ill-considered secession. Lincoln had made it clear that as President he was not leading his country in a conflict merely to abolish slavery, or to grind the Confederacy into a vassal society. Only that which he deemed essential to victory would be done. His stand against slavery was well known, but emancipation should come within the framework of united Government, if possible. Every move had to be made after painstaking deliberations; the President had to make certain that only the right step was taken at the right moment.

On July 22, 1862, Lincoln called a meeting of his Cabinet. The men of the Cabinet headed by William H. Seward, Secretary of State, gathered in his conference room on the second floor of the White House, as though for a routine meeting, which they assumed this to be. There had been many such discussions lately, all inconclusive, about the worsening news of the Civil War.

While the small group gathered, their taciturn chief, who at times seemed rude in his introspective moods, was quietly reading a book. Only after they had taken their seats did he seem to notice their presence, and look up from his book. Then he read a few paragraphs from it aloud. It was not a solemn treatise on war or statecraft, but a collection of the writing of Artemus Ward. They listened seriously, as though waiting for some solemn point to be made.

87

Lincoln looked at their serious faces and asked, "Gentlemen, why don't you laugh?" Then they laughed.

Lincoln picked up a sheet of notepaper on which he had written a few lines. He said, "I have called you on very important business; I have prepared a little paper of much significance." Then in an atmosphere of complete surprise he read it to them:

> . . . on the first day of January, in the year of our Lord one thousand eight hundred and sixty-three, all persons held as slaves within any state, or designated part of a state, the people whereof shall then be in rebellion against the United States, shall be then, thenceforward, and forever free. . . .

At that moment Lincoln, the country lawyer, the enigmatic President, asserted one of the awesome duties of the White House. It had already been established that in the White House rested the authority to conduct relations with foreign powers, to direct the actions that could lead to war, to speak for the *people* rather than for the Government as a power. Long ago Jackson had pointed out that only the President and his Vice President were elected by direct vote of all of the people, through their Electors. But never in history had any ruler assumed the authority to declare a race free at the expense of property owners.

It was not a statesman among those present, or one of the great "leaders," who first commented on the announcement. It was Postmaster General Blair who, acting as the President's conscience, commented on the draft. As a politician, he argued that such an order might adversely affect the Administration in the coming elec-

tions for seats in the House and one-third of the Senate in the following November. Who knew whether or not the majority of voters in the North, even though supporting the war to save the Union, might be stunned by this proclamation and lose trust in Lincoln?

Lincoln waved aside that argument. Then Seward commented that such a proclamation at this time might appear to North and South alike as "the last measure of an exhausted government, a cry for help." Why not wait until the Union had a victory in the field, something substantial enough to show that this was not part of the strategy of a government facing defeat?

Lincoln agreed to think it over, and the meeting adjourned. But in September he issued notice of the Proclamation, and on New Year's Day 1863 he called his Cabinet again into session. This was the day of the great annual "reception" for the public. It was held on schedule. For hours the crowds, shepherded by lines of soldiers, filed by and shook the President's hand.

At noon the reception line was terminated, and Lincoln went to his second-floor office. He was accompanied by all the Cabinet members except Seward. They had stood beside him at the reception. Seward came from the State Department, accompanied by his son Frederick, carrying a roll of embossed parchment, the Emancipation Proclamation.

Seward unrolled the parchment while a clerk prepared a clean quill pen for the President. Lincoln picked up the pen, and then put it down. He massaged his right hand with his left, tried a second

Painting of Lincoln reading the draft of the Emancipation Proclamation to his Cabinet

time to hold the pen, and again put it down. His advisors wondered if he was about to change his mind.

Then Lincoln looked up, smiled wryly, and surprised them with his explanation:

"I have been shaking hands since nine o'clock this morning and my right arm is almost paralyzed. If my name goes down in history, it will be for this act, and my whole soul is in it. If my hand trembles when I sign this Proclamation all who examine the document hereafter will say, 'He hesitated.'"

The President tried the pen again, and then boldly wrote his signature. He looked at it, turned to Seward and said, "That will do."

Of course, more actions by Lincoln than this would go down in history. But this was his first great step in asserting the latent powers of the President in war or emergency periods. The Proclamation was less important in Lincoln's personal history than in the new evidence it gave of the status of the White House. (Unremarked in the records of this historic moment was the fact that Lincoln carried through his plan despite the grief he must have felt over the death only eleven days earlier of William Wallace Lincoln, his second son.)

Longer and harder years were to try Lincoln the man—arguments with his 89

The Oval Room, which Johnson used as a library

President Andrew Johnson's private office

generals, who always delivered more excuses than victories, the bloodbaths over which he wept as determined and seasoned new military leaders fought to victories over equally determined opponents, visits to the wounded on Meridian Hill, inspection trips accompanied by a cavalry escort in yellow-piped uniforms—with whom rode little Tad, his son, in a copy of that uniform.

The great occasions made great moments—some of which seemed routine at the moment: the Gettysburg Address was a little talk reported in a minor position beside the great spread given in *The New York Times* to Henry Ward Beecher, speaking at the Brooklyn Academy of Music.

There would come the Second Inaugural Address, keyed to the theme of, "With malice toward none. . . . ," and announcement of the final victory at Richmond and Petersburg on April 3, 1865.

Of course, all the greatness was against a background of victory. With a few solitary exceptions, such as Robert E. Lee, defeat has few heroes. But here were victories, and the man and his actions—all combining to raise the White House to a pedestal that neither Washington nor Jefferson, ignorant of even the possibility of such circumstances, could have conceived.

The North looked to the White House as the custodian of victory, and the South looked to it as the base of understanding and merciful redemption. Even in his reelection, anticipating this victory, Lincoln had taken grave political risks to name as his running mate for the Vice President a Southerner from Tennessee who had re-

mained loyal but nonetheless had been Governor of that State in earlier days.

Of course, Andrew Johnson's election with Lincoln, to the Vice Presidency, was little more than symbolic, but it gave the White House a renewed glow as the center of power in the country after cessation of the War Between the States.

On the night of April 14, 1865, Lincoln was shot, dying of his wound the following day. He was the first President to be assassinated.

The new prestige, the authority, the leadership of the White House—all were threatened, and many asked if they could survive in the hands of the new President, while momentous questions arose with peace. The greatest of these questions concerned the actual power of the President *vis-à-vis* Congress. It would only be resolved by an attempt to impeach the President, and the failure of that impeachment by a single vote, a vote on which hung all the tradition of authority and prestige given to the White House by Washington, Jefferson, Jackson, and Lincoln.

In the eyes of the Congress, Johnson's greatest fault was his determination to carry out the policy of magnanimity toward the South reiterated by Lincoln. If he had been a Northerner, the task would have been easier, but he was a Southerner, and once in office a stubborn man.

In 1865 the Constitution strictly limited the sessions of Congress, which automatically ended on March 4, unless called into special session by the President. Lincoln had not called a special session and Johnson refused to do so. Therefore, during

The victorious Union Army being reviewed by President Johnson in 1865

the months of negotiation of peace and reconstruction, Congress could not meet, until the following December.

Arguing against his advisers, Johnson, perhaps too independently, appointed provisional governors for the former Confederate States, and he set the terms for the peace: renunciation of the Confederate debt to those countries that had aided the rebellion, ratification of the Thirteenth Amendment to the Constitution which abolished slavery, election of new Senators and Representatives, return to Constitutional forms and participation in the Union. All but Texas had complied with these terms before the Congress could meet in December.

What galled most the members of the Congress was a statement by Johnson:

A rebellious State, when it comes out of a rebellion, is still a State. I hold it a high duty to protect and to secure to those States a republican form of government, but such a State must be restored by its friends, not smothered by its enemies.

Such sentiments that seem realistic a century later were anathema to many in the Congress who wanted to share the glory and the patronage involved in "reconstruction." And the harshest critics were the most brilliant orators—Charles Sumner, Ben Wade, and Thaddeus Stevens. They preached the doctrine that the South was a conquered territory to be dealt with by the Congress. They termed the President presumptuous, dictatorial, and illegal in his views.

Through the winter of 1865–66, John-

Bird's-eye view of Washington in the 1860s. Engraving by Kimmell and Foster

son fought for the prerogatives of the White House. The two houses of Congress passed the law that established the Freedman's Bureau and a Civil Rights Bill, enfranchising Negroes immediately on the same footing with white persons. Johnson vetoed both measures as premature and passed without adequate preparation. Both were re-enacted over his veto.

An ill-tempered man, as far as politics were concerned, Johnson used the Presidency to lash back. In September, 1866 he accepted an invitation to speak at the laying of a cornerstone in Chicago for a monument planned in honor of Stephen A. Douglas. For the trip he laid out a route through Maryland, Pennsylvania, New York, Ohio, Indiana, Illinois, and Missouri—with speeches.

His theme was the Congress . . . "What has this Congress done? Have they done anything to restore the Union? No! On the contrary, they have done everything to prevent it. . . . I have been fighting traitors South. They have been whipped and crushed, and acknowledge their defeat. Now, I am fighting traitors North."

These were intemperate words, but likewise the times were intemperate. Also, in the North, where the political power lay, peace had brought such a surging prosperity that politics was left almost as a jousting field in which the contenders could fight it out, secure in their knowledge of little public questioning.

Johnson vetoed every law passed by Congress dealing with Reconstruction in the session that commenced in December 1866. The Congress in turn passed a resolution forbidding him to order any military action except through the General of

Probably the first photograph of the East Room, during the 1860s

the Army, Ulysses S. Grant. It passed over his veto another law forbidding the President to dismiss any official confirmed by the Senate, unless the Senate also approved the dismissal. In August 1867, with Congress in adjournment, Johnson dismissed Secretary of War Stanton. Congress returned in December and invalidated the dismissal. On February 21, 1868, Johnson fired him again.

These political charades seem in retrospect to be almost humorous byplays of politics, but the stakes were terrific—the very existence of the White House, of the Presidency, as a third and coordinate arm of the Government. And at last the Congress moved to use the ponderous machinery established in the Constitution for impeachment of a President on the grounds of "high crimes and misdemeanors."

In such an action, the House of Representatives acts as a court of inquiry. If a majority of the House votes for impeachment, the President must face trial before the Senate, sitting as a jury, with the Chief Justice of the United States as presiding officer.

Congress wasted no time. On March 5, 1868, trial for impeacment was voted by the House. The trial was begun, with Chief Justice Salmon P. Chase presiding. Thaddeus Stevens led the managers on the part of the House who presented the case for the prosecution. Henry Stanbury, Johnson's Attorney General, resigned in order to act as attorney for the defense.

Ninety witnesses were called in the thirty-day trial, as the prosecutors tried to break the back of the Presidency forever, to turn it into simply an administrative office under the control of the Congress. One vote decided the issue.

Fifty-four Senators cast secret ballots in the decision. Thirty-five cast votes of "guilty," but two-thirds, or thirty-six, were necessary to convict. Thus the White House rode out this storm.

Reconstruction continued harsh under the laws already passed by the Congress, but on Christmas Day 1868 Johnson pardoned Jefferson Davis and all other prisoners still held in punishment for rebellion and political offenses.

By then Grant had been overwhelmingly elected to the Presidency, and the White House again reflected the aura of "peace and prosperity" that some thought would last forever.

National Wing
EAST

EXECUTIVE RESIDENCE

J. D. Owen
Archt.

Official Wing
WEST

In the forty-seven years of Grant's life before he was elected to the Presidency in 1868, he had weathered as many ups and downs as had the White House in its somewhat longer history. Now the Presidency and the residence were thrown together at a new peak in their respective careers.

The election, held without much regard to the experience or fitness of the hero for the position, was another in the long lines of rewards for military heroes, but the hero was by all odds accidental and quite different from his fellow Presidents before and afterward.

Grant (whose official name was accidentally changed from Hiram Ulysses to Ulysses Simpson through a clerk's mistake in his nomination for West Point) had been a dashing member of his military class, adjudged the best rider in it. He was mentioned for distinguished service as a junior officer, only to be forced to resign for heavy drinking in 1852, at the age of thirty—an action ascribed to despondency over the hopeless outlook of a career in

which he could not support his family. In 1861, as a clerk in his brother's leather store who eked out a living by also peddling firewood, neither he nor his name would be recognized by any prominent leader North or South who heard it. Only the shortage of men with any military training prompted the State of Illinois to make him training commander of a hastily raised regiment of volunteers.

Four years later at Appomattox, the soldier from the frontier accepted the surrender of Robert E. Lee, who was fifteen years his senior, and in the time cycle of the Presidency Grant entered the White House. His first term is regarded as not brilliant but correct, due largely to his choice and support of Hamilton Fish as Secretary of State, his good relationship with the Congress, and the caliber of his recent military subordinates, including Generals William Tecumseh Sherman and Phil Sheridan.

All these felicitous circumstances enabled the events marking the progressive

Lithograph of General Ulysses S. Grant and his family

story of the White House to be set again with the mansion as the centerpiece of the tapestry rather than part of the background.

The White House was coming slowly into a position of recognition and respect, and for the first time its surroundings began to measure up to the formerly fanciful dreams of its designers. The nearby grounds and buildings took on forms that would be retained for almost a century—

forms that would be frantically preserved in more recent days only by a stemming of the tide of new architecture in modern Washington.

Externally the White House appeared then much as it does today, except that the office wings—then stables and service quarters—were lower. Its surroundings began to assume what later generations consider their traditional aspect. Instead of sitting in the center of an island of crude buildings and unkempt surround-

96

Wedding of Nellie Grant and Mr. A. C. F. Sartoris in the East Room, sketched by Harry Ogden

Amateur snapshots on the White House grounds

ings, the White House became an architectural jewel in a dignified setting. Grant got from Congress an appropriation of $13,000,000 with which to repair and improve the Capital. This was relatively easy in a boom economy after victory that saw the national debt which had reached a peak of more than $2,750,000,000 already being reduced by 1868 when he was elected.

To the east of the White House the massive Treasury Department Building

In the White House upstairs sitting room, the Hayes family has a musical evening led by Carl Schurz at the piano

soon was completed. West of the mansion an equally imposing building went up. The State, War and Navy Building's ultra-Victorian architecture contrasted sharply with the Greek Revival lines of the Treasury and the Federal of the White House. A mile to the east the Capitol gleamed in finished splendor, after seventy-five years, with its new dome.

Pennsylvania Avenue and other leading thoroughfares were paved with new surfaces, obliterating the ravages made by military columns. Pennsylvania Avenue was detoured north and west around the Treasury Building, to form a street along the north side of the White House grounds. This cut off a rectangle that had been part of the grounds, and the new area was named Lafayette Park. The little park was bordered by a number of older houses, including the one that had belonged to Dolley Madison, the one built by Decatur and St. John's Episcopal Church. Back of the White House, the Potomac swamps had been drained and the river accordingly pushed back a quarter of a mile. The old Tiber River, which had formed an open sewage drain from Capitol Hill all along Pennsylvania Avenue to the Potomac, was vaulted over, still used for the same purpose, but it was now underground.

Office-seekers in the lobby of the White House, awaiting an interview with President Hayes

In the Blue Room, President Hayes has the first official reception of a Chinese Minister to the United States

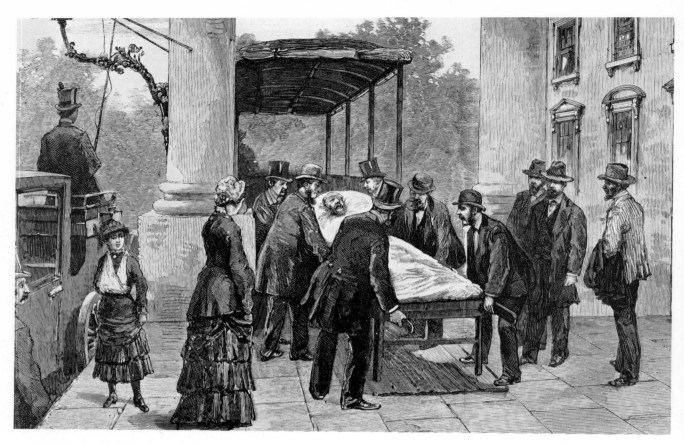

Removing the ailing President Garfield from the White House

Into this setting the victorious general moved. At the same time Congress raised his salary from the $25,000 provided for Presidents from the time of George Washington's Administration to $50,000 a year.

Using his additional income as President, without the need of a private fortune to spend on the office, Grant hired an Italian steward, Melah, to preside over state functions. When Grant's daughter, Nellie, married a young Englishman, Algernon Frederick Sartoris, the parlors were turned into bowers of flowers, and menus for the wedding banquet were printed on white satin. When Queen Victoria's youthful son, Prince Arthur, visited Washington, the White House banquet for thirty-five guests was reported to have cost $1,500.

In spite of its apparent affluence, the White House was hard-pressed in the aftermath of the war to hold its dominant position in the Capital. It was one among scores of opulent houses and, with its tinges of Southern aristocracy scrubbed away, it had lost its rather mystical claim to precedence.

No Virginia planter was seen in Washington, nor for that matter was any Southern accent heard in the conversation. Those Southern leaders who would have been welcomed shunned Washington because of the barbaric intensity of the changes forced by Reconstruction in the early post-Civil War years. And by an

The ornate Tiffany screen installed during Chester A. Arthur's Administration

Fireplace of the Red Room during Cleveland's tenure

inexplicable yet nonetheless observable change, the great wits and "names" of New England's intellectual aristocracy were notably absent. Living in obscurity, never invited to the official dinners, were two "radicals" of the time: Walt Whitman, the poet, who earned his living by a clerkship in the office of the Attorney General, and John Burroughs, the naturalist and Whitman's friend.

On the fringes of the greater Washington society, but not invited to the White House dinners, were a variety of individuals who made the city interesting but could not compete with the "new money." Ben Perley Poore was a famous journalist, and Joseph Medill of *The Chicago Tribune* was a rising light. So were C. L. Elliott, the portrait painter, and Edwin Forrest, the tragedian. Horatio King maintained a literary circle centering largely around his friend Henry Adams, the historian. But these were not the proud, the rich, and the predatory who formed the White House circle and who built the rich new houses on Connecticut Avenue, gambled at John Chamberlain's club, and gave dinners competing with the White

Another corner of the Red Room

The Blue Room

Northwest corner bedroom during Cleveland's stay at the White House

The Family Dining Room

The Harrison grandchildren in front of the White House

House menus at the restaurants operated by John Welcher and Sam Ward.

The hosts at these dinners were the White House guests and the setters of the new Washington pace: the winners of the California gold fortunes, the suppliers for the Civil War and the new trading society that won its wealth simultaneously in the West and in foreign enterprises. The money seemed to come so easily in commerce, and the President seemed to assume that all his friends were altruistic.

Perhaps it was a good thing for the White House that the worst scandals around Grant happened in 1869, at the beginning of his two terms. It made him cautious and helped preserve the integrity of his office.

Two of the financial predators of the era who had helped elect Grant were Jay Gould and James Fisk, Jr. They formed a plan to corner the gold market, and took into their association Abel R. Corbin, Grant's brother-in-law. The syndicate began to buy options for future delivery of gold from private dealers. The financial market woke up on September 1, 1869, to the fact that sellers were supposed

The Harrison grandchildren in the nursery

The Oval Room during Harrison's Administration was used both as the President's office . . .

. . . and as a family sitting room

A workman in the basement   *The upstairs office*

to cover syndicate orders amounting to $100,000,000, or six times the total of private gold holdings. In a few weeks the price of gold rose sharply and a "Black Friday" panic hit the trading centers.

When Grant finally ordered the Subtreasury in New York to begin selling gold in the open market, the panic broke, but much ruin had been caused. A Congressional investigation finally cleared Grant of any personal responsibility.

It was a nasty period in many ways. Secretary of War Belknap resigned under fire for collecting bribes. When the Credit Mobilier became a ruinous public fraud, members of the Cabinet and Congress were found to be broadly involved. There was exposure of the Whisky Ring, involving officials who, in return for bribes, cut collections of revenues owed to the Treasury by whisky distillers.

Grant more or less tottered out of his discredited Administrations, after publishing a notice that he would not stand for a third term. But he set an interesting precedent. In his last year of life, suffer-

ing from cancer, he wrote his biography as a means of providing his family with an estate—and his adviser and helper was Samuel Clemens (Mark Twain).

To the further honor of the White House, Grant in his later years refused to use bankruptcy as a refuge from his debts, including a note of $250,000 to W. H. Vanderbilt, and turned down an offer from P. T. Barnum of $100,000 plus a percentage of profits for the right to display Grant's medals and other souvenirs. There was stamina in the old White House yet—and every bit of strength that could be found was needed to withstand the wear and tear.

In the last quarter of the nineteenth century, the mansion became more and more the public's building by day and, according to the various ideas of its occupants, a token of the nation's formal dignity and prestige by night. These personalities were as varied as any cross-section of Americans could be.

After Grant came Rutherford B. Hayes, so Spartan in his simplicity that after leav-

The Harrisons were extremely proud of their White House conservatories

The State Dining Room

The State Bedroom

Family stairway

The Harrisons used the East Room as a reception room

ing office he felt it necessary to write a letter explaining that he had not made a "profit" from his salary as President. The rumors of miserliness were due in part to Mrs. Haye's widely publicized aversion to serving liquor or wine. Her nickname became "Lemonade Lucy."

James A. Garfield served only six months until he was assassinated by Charles J. Guiteau, an insane individual who thought he had been slighted in a bid for public office.

The accidental raising of Vice President Chester A. Arthur to the Presidency brought a set of grand airs into the mansion, which won public derision.

Then in the shifting political tides came Grover Cleveland, the first Democratic President after the Civil War, followed by Benjamin Harrison, Cleveland again, and William McKinley.

These years came close to seeing achieved what the Congress had failed to do in the impeachment proceedings against Andrew Johnson. The seat of power swung from the White House as Jefferson had defined it to a wide diffusion among State bosses and their spokesmen in Congress. The White House became a place for ceremonial occasions, official entertainment, and, except for rare actions, a public monument.

In 1865, his first year in office, Andrew Johnson spent $160,000 to refurnish the White House. By 1870, when a Congressional report was prepared on the decade from 1860, it was noted that "repairs and alterations" in that time had amounted to $95,250. In addition to Andrew Johnson's big splurge, in 1870 $46,053.02 was spent for "refurnishing"

and $27,000 for completing a new iron fence around the building. Repairs of Buchanan's conservatory made in the Grant period came to $28,000.

Some of these figures undoubtedly represent large profits added to costs in a day of contracting patronage unchecked by more recent budget and accounting reviews. Nonetheless, the White House took a heavy beating both from the traffic of people and from repeated "improvements."

The callers at the White House were legion, many with introductions issued in sheaves by members of Congress, others seeking jobs, and many merely curious. From October to June each year they walked without hindrance into the lower rooms of the mansion, where servants labored each night to repolish floors, to clean the furniture—and to count the number of missing small objects taken as souvenirs.

Uncounted numbers walked up the stairs from the reception hall to see the President or his secretaries, and to lounge in the chairs in the upper corridors and smoke. The living quarters of the Presidents' families had to be secured with locked doors to keep out the curious.

E. V. Smalley wrote that "the sighs of the disappointed office seekers for more than half a century have descended the steps, have permeated the walls, and give the air a quality that defies ventilation."

As if the air were not heavy enough, the redecoration from Andrew Johnson's time onward represented the low point in taste and the high mark in sheer weight and bulk. Gone were the more delicate French and early American pieces. In their place came the Victorian-type monstrosities of *115*

White House mounted messenger

When Mr. and Mrs. Hayes moved into the mansion, the President used five of the second-floor rooms for his offices, attended by six clerks and a messenger, and a Cabinet Room. The family, with three grown sons and two small children, had six bedrooms and a study. There was no room for a suite, and entertaining of a guest meant rearranging the family's ordinary sleeping quarters. Passage from some of the bedrooms to a bathroom required crossing the same hall that business callers had to use.

No member of the President's family could enter or leave the house privately. The round south portico opened only on the fenced lawn, with no gate to a street. Aside from a kitchen entrance and a servants' door in the basement, everyone had to use the formal entrance under the north portico built by Jackson—the same door that was open to every sightseer in Washington.

chests and bureaus and sofas, set against a background of dark paneling and heavy window hangings.

The ever-growing need for space for the President's offices, plus the installation of central heating fixtures and bathrooms forced partitions to be installed in areas where Hoban had not provided enough support, creating strains on every beam.

While the White House's roof was high and majestic, and the basement was deep, it had only two usable floors, except for kitchens in the basements. On the main floor the East Room, the State Dining Rooms, a family dining room and the three original formal parlors—always the Red, Green, and Blue Rooms—escaped partitioning changes.

From the time he "inherited the White House," although he knew from the political portents that he would never be elected President in his own right, Arthur paid more attention to the residence than to his political position. Following the taste of his times, he made the most sweeping changes between the Monroe Administration and the Kennedys, and he did it with the freedom of a bachelor, with Louis Tiffany's help.

Chester Arthur waited two and one-half months to move into the mansion. In the meantime, he spent more time with Colonel Almon F. Rockwell, Commissioner of Public Buildings and Grounds, than he did with political leaders. Like his bachelor or widowed predecessors, Van

116

Buren and Jackson, he managed his own housekeeping, although later he gave his sister, Mrs. Mary McElroy, the honorary position of housekeeper. He did not, however, allow her to take over. When Arthur occupied the mansion on December 7, 1881, after all the scrubbing, painting and refurnishing had been done, he arrived in a green landau, drawn by a pair of mahogany bay horses. The silver-mounted harnesss, the kersey lap robe, and the coachman's robe all were monogrammed "CAA."

This fat man, with an agreeable smile framed between long sideburns, auctioned everything that was in the way. First, there had been the cleaning out of the attic—twenty-four wagons of souvenirs that went to an auction that raised $3,000. Some of the "junk" included Monroe and Jackson furniture as well as later and more stolid things; also, Nellie Grant's birdcage and a pair of Lincoln's pants. The auction was held on April 15, 1882, and was attended by a crowd estimated at five thousand persons.

On the block went the entire furnishings of the East Room, "much of which was worn and moth-eaten, as also was the Green Room furniture." Also, marble-top tables, leather sofas, ottomans, old stoves.

Tiffany—whose name is perpetuated in the New York jewelry firm—gave the White House the same attention he was lavishing on the new and great houses of the rich, and took personal charge of this showcase job.

The great East Room assumed a less heavy air, with white walls, with the ceiling painted in silver with ivory trim. Draperies combining these shades were hung at the windows, and the new furniture was finished in brilliant contrasting colors. The Red Room was done in a deep shade of red with an interlacing frieze decorated with eagles and flags. The Blue Room was scaled down in shade to a robin's-egg tone, "with ornaments in a hand-pressed paper, touched out in ivory, gradually deepening as the ceiling was approached."

For the great piece of decoration, Tiffany designed and constructed a colored glass screen fitted between imitation marble columns, separating the East Room from the main entrance hall.

Arthur cared little for the State Dining Room, or for the occasional dinners that must be served there. He spent more time planning the smaller "family dining room," where about twenty guests could be served at dinners, having it decorated with heavy gold paper, with draperies of pomegranate plush at the windows.

In this new setting, for his brief period of time—in a peaceful lull throughout the world—"Chet" Arthur recaptured something of the atmosphere of the White House for which Thomas Jefferson had set a precedent. His was the leisurely life of a Chief of State separated from the worlds of politics or statecraft. From our vantage point in the twentieth century it seems like another world.

The President slept late, having his breakfast served between nine and ten. He forbade his staff to make engagements either on Sunday or Monday. From Tuesday through Saturday he received Senators and Representatives between ten and twelve. On Tuesdays and Fridays the Cabinet met at noon for an hour-long session. On the other business weekdays, *117*

Left: Frances Folsom Cleveland

Right: A drawing that appeared in Harper's Weekly *of the wedding of President Cleveland and Frances Folsom*

the noon hour was left open for hand-shaking with the public.

After lunch and a long rest period, the President kept appointments from four to five o'clock. From five to seven-thirty he rested, or read, or exercised, and dressed for dinner, which had been finally pushed back to the newer and fashionable evening period. Dinner, always with friends, might last until ten o'clock.

Quantities of food served had diminished, and perhaps the quality was better, but a sample menu of a small dinner served for friends—not dignitaries—in March 1882 showed that there were fourteen courses and six wines. In addition to the sumptuous dinners, fine entertainment was provided: prominent singers and artists such as Adelina Patti and her com-

pany, who gave one notable concert, and more popular entertainers such as the Fisk Jubilee Singers.

The idyl lasted until Inauguration Day 1885, when an unambitious Arthur rode with Grover Cleveland and turned his office over to a widowed and equally good-humored new President, who was holding back a rather surprising secret of his own, if in fact he had already made up his mind. The new President, forty-six years of age, had fallen in love with a twenty-one-year-old girl, just as he was entering his new office.

Her name was Frances Folsom. She was the daughter of a former law partner of Cleveland's, who had been killed in a traffic accident in 1875 and had named Cleveland as her guardian in his will,

while she was reared by her mother, Mrs. Oscar Folsom. Through the next ten years, until her graduation in 1885 from Wells College, Frances Folsom received letters, and eventually a bouquet for graduation day sent expressly from the White House greenhouse, from her "Uncle Cleve."

In the fall of 1885 the Washington official group first met Mrs. Folsom and her daughter, when as honored guests they shared with Miss Rose Cleveland, the President's sister, prominent places in the first White House reception line. During that visit, Cleveland proposed to Frances and at the same time urged her to "take a year to think it over." So she went abroad with her mother. But the thinking required less than a year.

In May 1886 Frances Folsom returned from Europe, with baggage including a trousseau purchased in Paris, to be met in New York by Secretary Thomas P. Lamont on behalf of the President. He hurried as soon as possible to see her, when a Memorial Day speech gave him an excuse to visit New York. In addition, Cleveland had to work out with Mrs. Folsom all the precedents involved in a White House wedding with the President as one of the principals. Cleveland might well be staking all his political future on this step. It could be extremely important to his growing political stature, so carefully tended during a term as Mayor of Buffalo, as Governor of New York, and now as a relatively new President. On May 29, before departing for the New York engage-

The east entrance to the White House

ment, Cleveland sent to members of his Cabinet and a few trustworthy personal friends a note he copied out himself:

I am to be married on Wednesday evening at seven o'clock at the White House to Miss Folsom. It will be a very quiet affair and I will be extremely gratified at your attendance on this occasion.

Sincerely yours—

At 5:30 A.M. on the wedding day, June 2, Miss Folsom and her mother arrived in Washington, to be met at the station and taken directly to the White House by Miss Cleveland. In his own quarters, the bridegroom-to-be breakfasted at eight, went through the motions of office business in the forenoon. After lunch he rode out in his coupe, driven by Albert Hawkins, for another look at a cottage on the Tennellytown Road which he had purchased for $21,500 as a private retreat only a few days earlier.

The guests arriving early for the wedding gathered in the East Room. The four mantels were banked with roses, orchids, and lilies; plants filled the fireplaces; smilax wreathed the chandeliers, and roses festooned the mirrors. Flowers also were banked in the Green and Red Rooms. In the Blue Room, site of the wedding, the flowers were less profuse, leaving room for the ceremony, where waited the Reverend Byron Sunderland, who performed it, and the Reverend William Cleveland, brother of the President, who blessed the couple.

Precisely at seven o'clock, church bells began to toll, the echoes of a salute rolled from the Navy Yard, and the Marine Band, mustered in the foyer, played Mendelssohn's Wedding March.

Hand in hand and unaccompanied, the only Presidential bride and bridegroom to be married in the White House walked into the Blue Room.

Miss Folsom was truly beautiful, and she handled with dignity a satin gown with a four-foot train and a five-foot wedding veil. The left hand of her long gloves was tucked back to leave her fingers free. On that hand the guests saw for the first time her engagement ring, set with a diamond and sapphires, and a diamond necklace around her throat which was her husband's wedding gift.

The couple departed immediately for Deer Park, Maryland, chosen as the site for a quiet honeymoon. However, their arrival attracted such a flood of tourists that they hastened back to Washington on June 9, to the relatively quiet White House and their new weekend cottage.

As the responsibilities and the staff of the Presidents grew the White House seemed almost to shrink. Mrs. Harrison, and later Mrs. Cleveland in her husband's second term after Harrison's, seriously complained that there was no privacy for family life, let alone room for house guests.

Their complaints prompted Colonel John M. Wilson, custodian of the White House grounds, to suggest in 1893 the erection of an office wing on the west terrace—the seemingly natural site that almost a century earlier had been used by Jefferson for his office "bower." But surprisingly in that era of bulging national prosperity, the Congress refused to appropriate the money for even repairing the encroaching wear and tear shown by the old building.

For years such a minor expense as keeping the now historic mansion in repair must come after other more popular items. The news headlines concerned the newer and always higher tariffs to protect American "infant industries," the growing conflict with Spain over the festering situation in Cuba, which prompted Harrison to start rebuilding the Navy with iron ships, and, finally, the explosion of the battleship *Maine* in Havana harbor. So again there was a war, with mobilization, slogans, and eventually a victory that only led to greater problems. But out of the confusion of the turn of the century came a new White House era.

William McKinley had only a few months to adjust to the Presidency after his Inaugural in 1897, and to begin working with the Congress that met in December of that year, when the conditions of Spanish occupation in Cuba reached the boiling point. The President, who had been elected on the basis of a comfortable agreement on domestic affairs within the Republican Party, found his office a whirlpool of argument.

John Hay, the Secretary of State—also journalist, poet, member of Abraham Lincoln's secretariat and diplomat—attempted to keep diplomacy on an even keel while urging a policy of American expansion in the Pacific. On none of these matters was the President very well informed, but he trusted Hay without taking definite steps to implement Hay's policies.

Neither McKinley nor Hay paid much attention at the time to the young man, addicted to the expression "Bully!" and with prominent teeth and blustering conversation, who had been slipped into the office of Assistant Secretary of the Navy. His patronage appointment was partly a bow to the aristocratic wing of the New York Republican organization and partly, it was freely commented, to get him sealed into a position where he would be least troublesome. However, he continued to talk, once remarking that "McKinley has no more backbone than a chocolate eclair."

When the *Maine* was sunk on February

15, 1898, the young official in the Navy resigned, got a political military commission which made him Lieutenant Colonel Theodore Roosevelt, Jr., and raised a cavalry regiment of volunteers who called themselves the "Rough Riders." Few persons even realized that the quiet, efficient, and distinguished Colonel Leonard Wood was their actual commander.

"Teddy" got the headlines all the way from training camp to the charge up San Juan Hill in Cuba. . . . And in the election of 1900 it was Teddy who edged his political way up to the post of the Vice Presidency, again relegated to a quiet position, but on Inaugural Day in 1901 he stood removed from the White House by only six months and ten days.

On September 14, 1901, McKinley died from an assassin's bullet and Theodore Roosevelt became master of the

mansion. At the age of forty-two, the politician who had been sidetracked by his bosses after storming through the offices of Police Commissioner of New York and the New York Governorship, in the post-Spanish-American war period, became the new voice and representative of the twentieth century in the White House.

He was the youngest President up to his time, inheritor of a small and scattered new empire garnered by Secretary Hay, and the first President to introduce into the house a brood of his own young children. It was typical of Teddy's Presidency that he received news of McKinley's assassination at a remote mountain camp in upper New York. He rode horseback ten miles down a trail on Mount Tahawus, and drove forty miles by buggy to the nearest railroad station where he could catch a train for New

Three stereoscope pictures of the White House during McKinley's Administration. From left to right: the Cabinet Room, the Old Oak Room, and the State Bedroom

York, and take the oath of his new office.

At the oath-taking, Roosevelt pledged himself "to continue absolutely unbroken the policy of President McKinley for the peace, prosperity, and honor of our beloved country." And by his own lights he did, but within a year the last traces of the attitudes and many of the customs of the older century were gone.

The American people had not elected Roosevelt to his mastership of the House, but when he inherited it they liked him—his down-to-earth manner of speaking to the public, combined with his aura of absolute confidence inherited through generations of assured and wealthy ancestors, including founders of the Union Club and the Museum of Natural History.

With public mourning for the assassinated McKinley completed, Theodore Roosevelt opened the White House officially in his own way on New Year's Day

1902—with a "bang" that never ceased to reverberate during his years of residence there. This was the New Year's Reception for the public, during which the President's stamina was genuinely tested while he shook the hands of eighty-one hundred people.

Allowing only one day for the staff to clear away the debris and trackings of that reception, the next night the President gave a dinner for his Cabinet. Beside the new President stood his second wife, while in the background hovered his children —his daughter Alice by his first wife and his sons by his second.

On the third night of the New Year there was a reception, a buffet supper in the State Dining Room, and dancing in the East Room. The occasion was the debut of Alice, who thereafter was known in Washington as "Princess Alice."

Among the guests it is possible that 125

The kitchen during the McKinley Administration

The laundry

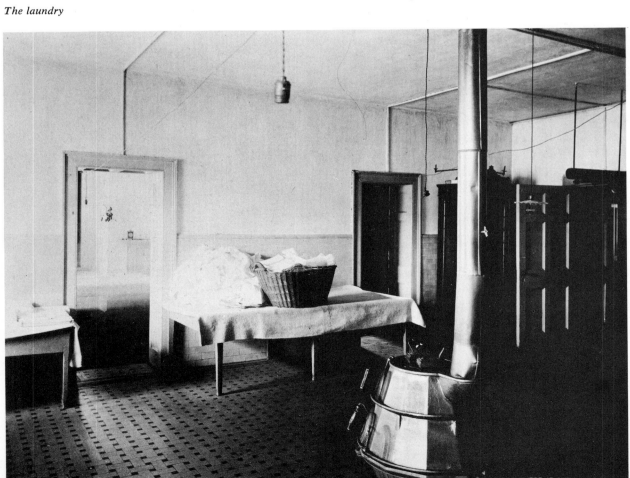

there were also two Roosevelt cousins, who were frequent visitors to the mansion but who were completely outshone by the more glamorous Presidential family. One was the President's niece, Eleanor, daughter of his deceased brother Elliott, over whom he watched with a fatherly interest. The other was a fourth cousin, Franklin Delano Roosevelt, then a twenty-year-old student and a family friend.

However, if the supercharged Theodore Roosevelt seemed intent on altering the social pace of the White House, he seemed just as intent on raising the Presidency to a position of leadership in modern political philosophy, and at the same time putting his own imprint on the building.

The Presidency itself jumped several notches in prestige under Theodore Roosevelt's impetuous leadership. He became a headline figure in his campaigns to "bust the trusts," to protect labor's rights, and at the same time censuring strikes marked by illegal violence. In the international field, he helped settle the Russo-Japanese War, pushed through construction of the Panama Canal, and threatened Germany with war under the Monroe Doctrine if it carried through plans to occupy Venezuela over a matter of unpaid debts.

So determined was the leadership of this new man in the White House that he forced through modernization of the buildings, with addition of an office wing, at a cost of more than $500,000 with all of the work completed between June 20, 1902, when Congress appropriated the money, and October, when that year's official social season opened.

There was some talk of providing the President with another house as a residence and retaining the White House as an executive office building, now that the President's staff had grown to thirty persons. But Teddy Roosevelt flatly turned down such a proposal.

The work was entrusted to the firm of McKim, Mead, and White, which moved an army of workmen into the grounds with the avowed purpose of preserving all the traditional flavor of the old house, while substituting a modern dwelling within the walls. All that remained of what Hoban had created were those outer walls and two marble mantelpieces.

For the architectural firm, headed by the celebrated Stanford White, the contract actually was fairly small in comparison to the many great mansions and office buildings included in its work. But it was a prestigious contract, with *carte blanche* written into the appropriation bill: "for repair and refurnishing the Executive Mansion for each and every purpose connected therewith, including all necessary alterations and repairs, cabinet work, decoration of rooms, covered ways and approaches, grading, paving porte-cocheres, gates and electric wiring and light fixtures for house and grounds."

The office wing on the west—the site of Jefferson's original wooden structures—was a one-story addition with "a Cabinet room, a President's office and retiring room, offices for two secretaries, a telegraph and telephone room, a large room for stenographers, a room for the press, a main hall to be fitted as a reception room, file rooms and closets in the basement." Then $10,000 was authorized for new furniture for these offices. And when the office wing was connected by a covered 127

Offices next to the President's office

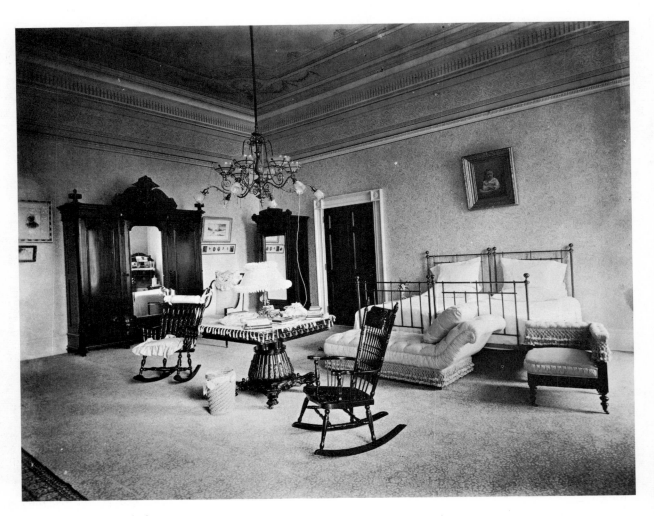

President McKinley's bedroom

Coaches lined up in front of the White House awaiting guests

walkway with the main house, the Buchanan greenhouses finally disappeared.

The importance of this restoration of the White House rested on two factors. First, the decision was made to recapture the original inspiration of the building before scattered and yellowing records disappeared forever, as they might easily have done in the growing disorganized state of the Government archives. Then, for the first time architects of vision not swayed by current fads took on the assignment.

This restoration in 1902 therefore left a legacy that might not have been recapturable fifty years later when the next great step was to be taken, with perpetuation in more permanent materials of the mansion.

Excerpts from the reports of the period illustrate the painstaking care taken, for which a nation is grateful:

The preliminary examination of the White House shows that the portion devoted to the President's offices is in an unsafe condition [in the original house], and that radical steps should be taken to relieve the beams from the weight they have carried too many years. Also, that in order to put the house into shape for occupancy under modern requirements, bathrooms, and so forth, must be provided in the various suites of chambers. The original house was built simply, and well built, considering the limited amount of money then available for public buildings in Washington; but the changes that have been made from time to time have resulted in a medley of styles, none of which is of a permanent character.

The preliminary survey contemplated merely putting the house in order and making it safe. There was no consideration given at that time to more ample provisions for large dinners and for accommodations for the large public receptions. A study of the historic White House, however, and the discovery in the Library of Congress of old prints and plans of the house,

shows that by a return to the original design the White House can be put into such a condition that it will serve every use intended for many years to come, and that the increased demand for rooms in the house can be met in a dignified and satisfactory manner at a cost which is small when compared with the cost either of a new residence or of additions to the present building, both of which are objectionable from many points of view.

The original plans for the White House show porticoes on the West and on the East, extending 150 feet from the main building. These porticoes contain servants' quarters, the laundry, store rooms and house offices generally. The western portico remains, and forms a foundation for the present conservatory. These porticoes are at the garden level on the South, while on the North the roofs reach only to the level of the driveway. Unfortunately the space south of the western portico has been filled by glass houses for plants and much of the room in the portico has been used for potting plants and like work. Architecturally this portico is finely constructed, with a row of dignified stone columns supporting the roof. The vaulting and general construction show that the portico was considered an integral portion of the house, and by reason of having a southern exposure the rooms therein are very desirable.

The restoration of the West Portico to its original uses and the replacing of the East Portico will relieve the main building of a number of the domestic offices and make available for public purposes more than half of the garden floor [now known as the basement]. On occasions of large receptions carriages would enter the ground at a point near the fountain, opposite the west front of the Treasury Building. Alighting under a porte-cochere, the people, protected from the weather, would walk under an arcade to the house proper. Entering at the doors under the East Room, they would find ample dressing rooms to the right and left.

The porticoes were built, but not without problems, as a progress report made clear:

After the removal of the pipes which are now hung from the ceiling the corridor would be both ample in size and dignified in appear-

East Room flora at the beginning of Teddy Roosevelt's Administration

The temporary White House on Jackson Place used by the Roosevelts while the Presidential mansion was being rebuilt in 1902

Stereoscope picture of the White House from the Washington Monument, 1902

ance. From this corridor a stone stairway fifteen feet wide would lead to the main floor, which would be available for all receptions. The elimination of exposure on the front portico and the doing away with the undignified crush occasioned by turning the main hall into a dressing room on reception occasions are the advantages to be gained by the change.

On leaving a reception five hundred people could be sheltered under the East Portico while waiting for their carriages and the porte-cochere would be sufficient to allow the approach of three carriages at a time. In this connection it may be noted that a separate entrance and separate dressing rooms under the Blue Room are provided for special guests, thus avoiding confusion on occasions of ceremony.

The elimination of the executive offices from the White House gives an opportunity to rearrange the house as a residence for the President. The President retains a room in which he would see callers at hours when he is not in his office. The main hall becomes a spacious and dignified reception room. The East Room is to be rebuilt, the floors made safe, and a new plan for decoration adopted. By the removal of the present private staircase the State Dining Room will be enlarged by about sixty per cent of its present size, and the problem of giving large dinners will be solved for a number of years to come.

The principles on which the restoration will be done are these:

To put the house in the condition originally planned but never carried out.

To make the changes in such manner that the house will never again have to be altered; that is to say, the work will represent the period in which the house belongs architecturally, and therefore be independent of changing fashions.

To modernize the house insofar as the living rooms are concerned and provide all those conveniences which are now lacking.

Upon approval of these ideas, the work progressed after some ruthless cleaning out of the transient fads such as the Tiffany glass screen. It seemed that within only a score of years American taste had matured, and the White House became a shining example.

Here, told more graphically than is possible in any paraphrase, is how it was done:

On making as careful an examination of the White House as was possible while the house was occupied, it was found that the entire lower floor was used for house service. The principal rooms at the northeast corner were occupied by the laundry; the central rooms on either side of the main corridor were used for the heating and mechanical plants; the kitchens occupied the northwest corner; and much of the remainder of this floor was occupied by storerooms and servants' bedrooms.

Of the floor of the first story, those under the main hall, the private dining room, and pantry were found to be in good condition. The floor under the central portion of the East Room showed marked settlement due to overloading and to heating coils on the ceiling underneath. The base of the room gave evidence of the settlement of the floor, and the same was true in the Green and Blue Rooms. The floor of the State Dining Room, while not showing settlement, was so insufficiently supported as to cause dishes on the sideboard to rattle when the waiters were serving, and the plastering below was badly cracked from excessive vibration.

At large receptions, when potted plants were brought in from the greenhouses and when the house was filled with people it was the custom to put shores under the floors of the East Room, the State Dining Room and the main hall at both ends for safety.

The fine, groined arches of the basement had been cut into in all directions to accommodate heating and plumbing pipes. These old vaulted ceilings are of brick and stone.

The heating chamber, which contained the coils of the heating apparatus, has been built into the main corridor. The fresh air duct and the heat mains were suspended from the corridor ceiling, the masonry arches having been cut away in consequence. The whole ground floor was in bad condition; there was about it a general air of delapidation, and the woodwork particularly was out of repair.

There was scarcely a room in the house in which the plaster was in good condition. In a number of instances as many as five layers of paper were found, and when the paper was removed the plaster came also.

The second floor showed such a degree of settlement as to make an entire new floor necessary. The floors of the room devoted to the offices, also the library, were so insufficient that steel beams were required. The enlargement of the State Dining Room by the removal of the north wall of the room, which wall carried the floor beams of the upper stories, made it necessary to build a heavy steel truss in the attic from which the second floor is suspended.

The attic, occupied by servants, was reached only by the elevator. It is true that from the attic there was a narrow winding stairway leading to a mezzanine floor adjacent to the elevator; and from this mezzanine floor a swinging iron ladder led down from a trapdoor directly in front of the elevator—a most dangerous arrangement in case of fire.

The roof drainage had been carried through the roof, and thence on top of the attic floor to central points, descending to the ground through the house itself. The conductors were troughs hollowed out of logs. These troughs have been replaced with wrought-iron pipes carried down along the external walls. The roof itself, which, under a fresh coat of paint, appeared in good condition, was found to be in such bad shape as to require almost entire renewal.

135

From left to right: a reception of distinguished guests; President Roosevelt at his daughter Alice's wedding to Nicholas Longworth; Teddy Roosevelt's Red Room

At first it was thought that the old heating apparatus could remain, at least in large part. Upon further examination, however, it was found that only by removal of all the duct work and heating coils, which were suspended from the ceiling through the ground floor, could this floor be made available for any uses other than those of service.

The removal of ducts and so forth, involved lowering the boiler and placing all pipes and ducts in trenches under the floor. The change necessitated a large unexpected expenditure, but in return the finely proportioned room under the Blue Room has become a reception room for guests of honor, and ample dressing room accommodations not only for all these guests but for all the guests at public receptions have been added.

The electric wiring was not only old, defective and obsolete, but actually dangerous, as in many places beams and studdings were found charred for a considerable distance about the wires where the insulation had completely worn off. Where wires have been carried through wood joists a porcelain insulating tube is usually placed through the beam, and the wire threaded through that, but in the White House, in very many cases, the only protection was the

insulation on the wire itself, and that had been worn off by contact with the rough timber.

The entire wiring system is now in accordance with the very best modern practice, all wires being run through wrought-iron pipes so that if at any future time the wires should be burned out or in any way damaged they can be withdrawn and new ones put in without causing the slightest damage. New cables and conduits were also carried across the street to the State, War and Navy Building. These were not contemplated, and there was no appropriation for work beyond the grounds. This was a very costly item. . . .

A new standpipe with fire hose has been provided running from the ground floor to the attic and carried outside the house to a point which is accessible to the city fire department, so that in case of fire the attic of the house has the same fire protection as a modern office building.

The old filter, though of good type, was too small, and has been replaced with one of much greater capacity. The old filter has been placed in the office building.

Trees for the east and west terraces have been purchased by contract and will be in not later than May 1.

In short, it was necessary to reconstruct the interior of the White House from basement to attic in order to secure comfort, safety and necessary sanitary conditions.

The east and west terraces are first found on a plan drawn by Latrobe in 1807. The west terrace had degenerated into workshops connected with the various greenhouses that had been constructed from time to time in such a manner as not only to take away from it light and air, but entirely to conceal it. The east terrace was removed sometime prior to 1870. This terrace has been rebuilt in a substantial manner, with the addition of a porte-cochere opposite the Treasury Department. In excavating for the new terrace wing, the foundations of the old one were discovered. A semi-circular drive leads to the new entrance, which now is used on all occasions of large entertainment. The porte-cochere, which is glassed in during winter, is flanked by watchmen's quarters, thus doing away with the small wooden pavilion on the grounds. The east terrace is occupied by coat rooms, containing boxes for 2,500 wraps, umbrella stands and other conveniences, thus doing away with the necessity of pressing into service as cloakrooms the main hall of the State and private dining rooms.

In the house proper, more than one-half of the lower floors is given up to dressing rooms, with toilet rooms attached, conveniences heretofore entirely lacking. The removal of the pipes from the corridor gives a spacious passageway dignified by the fine architectural features constructed by Hoban. Decorated with portraits and plants, and finished with sofas and large chairs, the corridor is made comfortable for those who wish for an opportunity to enter the lines formed for the receptions.

A stone floor has been laid, and a broad and easy flight of stairs leads to the main floor of the house. The kitchen has not been changed materially, but a new refrigerating room and many other conveniences have been added.

The west wing now accommodates the laundry and ironing rooms, the maids' dining room, and separate quarters for men and women servants, with ample toilet arrangements of the most approved pattern.

The removal of the greenhouses, besides adding materially to the healthfulness of the White House, has restored to the south front of the building that sense of dignity of which during the past forty years it has been deprived by the various encroachments. The fine colonnades on the south front of the terraces, now restored, *137*

Roll call of the White House police . . . including Archie and Quentin Roosevelt

Children's party on the White House lawn, given by Taft

Taft at his White House desk signing the New Mexico and Arizona statehood bill, 1912

President Taft greeting members of society at a White House reception

once more give to the White House the long base from which the main structure rises with great architectural effect.

The main floor is devoted to what may be termed the state apartments, as opposed to the rooms given over to the family life of the President's household. The only family room on this floor is the private dining room, and even to this the family has access on formal occasions.

Every room on this floor had been completely remade and refurnished.

The floor and the base of the wainscot of the main hall and corridor are of Joliet stone, the floor being waxed. The walls and ceilings have been replastered, the colors being buff and white. Six columns take the place formerly occupied by the colored glass screen. Two large tubs of Istrian stone, filled with plants, fill the spaces between the columns on either side of the central opening. Two mirrors reaching from the floor to the ceiling occupy portions of the east and west wall space; and it is suggested that as soon as may be practicable replicas of Houdon's statue of Washington, at Richmond, and of Saint-Gaudens' statue of Lincoln, at Chicago, be placed in front of these mirrors.

Bronze standards carrying clusters of electric lights, and a bronze lantern furnish the light for this room; and a bronze and glass vestibule offers protection at the least expense of light. The curtains, and the rug, 70 feet in length, which carpets the corridor from the doors of the State Dining Rooms to those of the East Room, are deep crimson in color.

Directly beneath the lantern, the President's seal appears in yellow bronze in the stone floor, and the pavement between the central columns carries in bronze the dates 1792–1902, inscribed in an ellipse of 45 stars.

The changes made in the State Dining Room necessitated the removal of two marble mantels that are contemporary with the house itself. Exquisitely carved in London and imported with others purchased for the Capitol, these mantels were almost the only historic furnishings of the White House at the time when the restoration began. Too small for the spaces where they were placed, they now become the chief ornaments of the Red and Green rooms, respectively. The wainscoting of the Red Room is in white enamel and there is a new cornice. The wall coverings and the curtains are of red velvet, and the furniture is upholstered in red damask. There is a crystal chandelier and side lights; new andirons, a new mirror between the windows, and an antique rug.

Rarely beautiful in its proportions, the Blue Room has been made notable by the events that have taken place within its walls; and in the changes particular emphasis has been placed on this room. The mantel is of pure white marble, the shelf being supported on bundles of arrows carved in white marble with bronze tips and feathers; the wainscoting is in white enamel; the wall covering is of heavy, corded, blue silk, on which is embroidered at top and bottom the Grecian fret; the curtain hangings, of the same material as the wall covering, are embroidered with stars, and the curtain poles are surmounted by gilt eagles. The Grecian fret appears also in the ceiling. The furniture is in white and gold, upholstered in blue and gold.

Blind doors have been cut in the walls near the southern end of the room, and at receptions the guests coming from the Red Room pass the

139

receiving party standing in a single line directly in front of the windows. The guests especially invited to share the Blue Room with the receiving party now face the President instead of being at his back as formerly, and a silken cord stretched across the room from door to door insures freedom of passage for the guests while being presented.

In the Green Room the wall covering and curtains of green velvet are copied from an old piece of Genoese velvet; the marble console table shares with the mantel the distinction of age and grace; the furniture—upholstered in tapestry—the rug, the mirror, the andirons, the crystal chandeliers and side lights, all are new.

The walls of the East Room are covered with wood paneling, enameled; the ornamental ceiling is done in stucco, and set into the walls are twelve low relief panels by Piccirilli Brothers, sculptors, the subjects being taken from Aesop's Fables. On each of the east and west sides of the room are two mantels of colored marble, with mirrors over them and candelabra on the shelves. The crystal chandeliers form constituent parts of the decoration, as do also the four bronze standards bearing electric lights, which are placed at the four corners of the room.

The window draperies are of heavy yellow damask; the banquettes are gilded and carved and are covered with silk velours, and there are four new console tables with marble tops. In this room, as in the other rooms on the drawing-room floor (except in the hall, where stone is used), hardwood floors have been laid, and wainscots have been introduced, of which the lower member has been made of marble of suitable color. The concert grand piano, decorated by Dewing, is the gift of the makers.

By renewing the partition and including the western end of the corridor, the State Dining Room has been enlarged by over sixty per cent, and instead of accommodating between fifty and sixty guests at table, one hundred and seven can be seated. A stone chimney-piece, with an antique fire-set, has been added. The walls are paneled from floor to ceiling in oak, richly carved; the chandelier and wall branches are of silver, and heads of American game are used around the frieze. The ceiling, in stucco, is elaborately decorated. There is an India carpet in solid color, the table and sideboards are of mahogany, and the chairs are upholstered in tapestry. The draperies are in green velvet. Two tapestries, one bearing a text from Virgil's VIII Eclogue, are of Flemish work of the Seventeenth Century.

From the State Dining Room, as also from the East Room, windows open on the restored terraces, which are to be ornamented with suitable trees and fountains, and made comfortable with garden chairs and tables. These two garden-like spaces, 160 by 35 feet each, not only restore the area formerly occupied by the conservatory, but double it in extent.

A vaulted ceiling and wall paneling in plaster, a new marble mantel, a wainscoting in white enamel, a mirror copied from one belonging to the White House period, a mahogany table, chairs and sideboard, all made from special designs, are features of the private dining room.

To the butler's pantry a special mezzanine has been added, and all dressers and interior fixtures have been entirely renewed, the storage space now being more than double what it was before the alterations were made. An electric plate warmer has been provided, and a new electric dumb-waiter from the kitchen to the mezzanine story of the butler's pantry; also new ventilating apparatus.

The usher's lobby has been entirely renewed and refitted with new wainscot, wall covering, floor, rug, furniture and curtains.

Extending from basement to attic is a marble and iron staircase and an electric elevator running up through a fireproof hall. In connection with the elevator it is interesting to note that a part of the oak woodwork in the new elevator-car was made from roof trusses of the Old South Church in Boston, which in its day sheltered the Boston Tea Party. Moore Norcross had had the timbers in his yard since the time he replaced the old roof of the church with a new one.

The main stairway to the second floor is of Joliet stone, and consists of a broad flight from the main floor to the landings, where it divides into two flights. The railing is of forged iron and brass, with hand rail covered with velvet. A double gate of wrought iron, which rolls back into double pockets in the walls, has been placed at the foot of the staircase. Above the landing the walls are paneled and painted.

Originally it was the intention not to touch any of the bedrooms except those over the East Room. It was found, however, that the electric wiring was in such bad condition that it would have to be entirely renewed. It then became necessary to cut the plaster in all of the rooms in order to get in the new electric ducts. This made it essential to repaint or redecorate every room.

The space given up to executive clerks was made into two suites of bedrooms, each having its separate bathroom. A low wood wainscoting and new wood mantels were placed in the four large bedrooms and a new marble mantel in the President's study [formerly known as the Cabinet Room]. The new floors are of white maple. In the four large bedrooms the new wood mantels, the wainscoting and the wood paneling are all very simple in character.

New furniture has been provided for the four new rooms over the East Room, while for the remaining rooms on this floor the old furniture has been used, but has been re-covered with materials to match the new curtains which have been provided for all rooms except the library. New electric-light fixtures have been provided, as it was found that with very few exceptions the old fixtures were not fit to use again. New carpets have been laid in the rooms over the East Room and in the President's study, and the old carpets have been re-cut and made up for the remaining rooms. All the bathrooms have been furnished with marble floors and tiled walls, and the fixtures are the best.

In connection with the second-floor rooms, it should be noted that the large increase in the cost of electric wiring and the heating plants, amounting to some $13,000, which at the beginning could not have been foreseen, made it necessary to cut down the amounts allowed for interior finish, furniture, and decoration by a like amount.

On the President's instructions, the structural parts and the finish of the public rooms on the drawing-room floor were made the first consideration, and for this reason new furniture and carpets were provided for only the bedrooms over the East Room. The library, which is the family living room, has scarcely been touched; in fact, nothing was done excepting what was absolutely necessary to make good after the new electric wiring of the room. In the President's study the walls are covered with plain buckram, and new bookshelves of the simplest character have been provided.

The corridor walls have been covered with

burlap, and the ceilings and the woodwork have been painted.

The old iron balustrade has been removed from the north front of the White House, and has been replaced by a stone balustrade. The lanterns which disfigured the great columns of the North Portico have been removed, and that portico is now lighted by a single bronze lamp suspended from the roof of the portico.

An important point is the new system of service. Under the old conditions, the butchers' and bakers' wagons drove up to the north front of the house on the level with the main floor, and supplies were carried down the area steps and into the building in that way. Under present conditions all supplies enter at the east entrance on the ground floor level, the wagons driving under the North Portico and never coming into view. When the temporary office shall have been removed, the service may be improved still further by constructing a passageway for the wagons from the east side of the grounds to the west of the garden level.

. . . the Executive Office was finished on September 30 and occupied about the middle of October. The family floor of the White House was reoccupied on November 4; on December 18 the first official function, a Cabinet dinner, took place in the restored White House, and on January 1, 1903, the East Terrace was used for the first time, a full month in advance of the date set for completion of this portion of the work.

The changes have been made within the appropriations of Congress, and a balance of $7,906.10 is available for additional furnishings.

So the White House was rebuilt for "all time to come"—so it was thought in 1902. And although it had been called the White House informally for almost a century, Theodore Roosevelt made the name official. This was the name he now had engraved on the President's stationery.

On February 17, 1906, Theodore Roosevelt gave a White House wedding for his daughter Alice, when she was mar-

The State Dining Room decorated for a special party

ried to Nicholas Longworth, a wealthy Congressman from Ohio, who in time and seniority would become Speaker of the House—Republican, of course.

This wedding followed by almost a year another for which Teddy visited New York on March 17, 1905, in order to "give the bride away," when Eleanor, his niece, married Franklin Delano Roosevelt, a law student and resident of Hyde Park, New York.

While the changes in the White House under Theodore Roosevelt were not as permanent as the architects optimistically predicted they would be, they were the best up to their time. For that matter, the basic plans and the external appearance endured very well.

In the meantime, perhaps because of Teddy's rambunctious Administration, the whole atmosphere of the White House subtly changed from the attitude of semi- 143 apology some recent Presidents had brought to it into one of self-confidence.

Bickerings in Congress over the cost of the establishment ceased to be matters of public argument. In addition to the larger salary given to the President, there were added other prerogatives. The staff of the White House in service was put on Government expense, with the rather ludicrous exception that the President should pay for all of the food eaten by the help, as well as supplying lunch for the police guards on duty there. (Much later Calvin Coolidge attempted to curb this expense, reporting to the public that the food bill for the household was $2,500 a month, which he felt was high.)

And the White House finally achieved that mark of prestige which was becoming common among the millionaires in the new era of prosperity—an ocean-going yacht. This was *Mayflower,* recommissioned by the Navy after the Spanish-American War from among a fleet of vessels pressed into service in that affray. A fairly large ship, painted white, she was an impressive vessel, but with a tendency to roll heavily in any but the calmest of waters. But the ship was an elegant adjunct for weekends on the quiet Potomac River. Theodore Roosevelt considered the yacht his favorite toy, and entertained lavishly aboard her. As a note of the times, he required all men boarding her as guests—regardless of the heat of Washington summers—to wear Prince Albert coats and top hats.

Mayflower finally was junked in an economy move when the Great Depression occurred after 1929, but she stands out as a breaking-point in the manner in which the United States treated occupants of the White House. After a century in which the White House had been a financial burden to its occupants, the commissioning of this one yacht, with its crew of approximately fifty men, maintenance, and special escort—all hidden deep in the Navy budgets—might well have cost as much as the comparable costs of staffing and maintaining the White House itself.

When Theodore Roosevelt turned over the White House on March 4, 1909, to William Howard Taft, history in the form of world-shaking events was virtually standing still, and the jovial new President settled gracefully into a mansion that for its day was the peak of sophistication and elegant comfort.

Roosevelt went off on a tour of Europe, hunted big game in Africa, and edited the magazine *Outlook.* Taft settled down to be a conservative President, but his espousal of outdated positions such as the high tariff wall erected by the United States would wreck his Administration within four years and help to tear apart the Republican Party. The White House never sits far away from political controversy.

In its developing maturity in the first two decades of the twentieth century, about the only thing that the White House was not protected against was political accident. From 1912 onward these "accidents" happened with surprising rapidity in what appeared to be the still-placid Southern atmosphere of the mansion on the Potomac.

They began with a split in the Republican Party that brought the first Southern-born President in to the White House since Andrew Johnson's Administration;

they ended temporarily with White House-Senate conflict that wrecked all hope for the League of Nations and saw a strong-willed woman assuming virtual guardianship of a paralyzed President.

Yet after a little while the White House emerged with extraordinary new authority, even though its prestige was a little tarnished.

When Theodore Roosevelt welcomed William Howard Taft as his successor, neither guessed that within two years the former would begin to pull down the

The mansion blanketed in snow

latter's leadership and broach the practice under which no prior President had run for a third term. Yet, in his fight against the "conservatism" of Taft's Administration, and backed strongly by famous Republicans, including Charles Evans Hughes and Henry L. Stimson, Roosevelt tried it.

The upshot of his formation of the Bull Moose Party, with its splitting of Republican strength, sent to the White House the scholarly Woodrow Wilson—Virginia native, later President of Princeton University and Governor of New Jersey. Wilson was elected in 1912 on the basis of his scholarly prestige and his own liberal views; he would survive to lead his country in its first major foreign war and to exert dictatorial rights for a while under those war powers.

Wilson's Inaugural was the signal that the personality of the White House, typified in each successive President, would be quite different from anything in living memory. Some saw in his expression and the Calvinistic solemnity of his ancestry a stern resolve to be a "reform" President in domestic affairs.

The house attained an even more solemn air due to the semi-invalidism of Wilson's first wife, who lived only until 1914, and the studious if not antisocial bearing of their daughters. There was little time for the type of levity or activities such as the bumptious Theodore Roosevelt family had contributed.

When war in Europe broke out in 1914, the White House became an even more serious planning center. This changed very little in 1915, when Wilson married the matron, Mrs. Edith Bolling Galt, whose interests were more dedicated to her husband's actions in the Presidency than to social affairs. Neither change nor adjustment in the White House routine interfered or was permitted to interfere with the office work. The house became cold, and Wilson's initial contribution of scholarly distinction wore so thin that he squeaked through re-election by a margin so narrow that only a count of California's votes on the second day after national balloting confirmed his victory for a second term. Perhaps it was harder than later generations realize to generate enthusiasm behind leadership for a proposed League to Enforce Peace while Europe was in flames, or to win a political campaign with the slogan, "He kept us out of war."

Furthermore, when Wilson spoke to crowds—and he could speak to them only face to face in the days before sound newsreels, radio, or television—his voice was the cold, twangy one of a lecturer voicing facts, not that of an inspired leader.

Yet when war engulfed the United States only a few weeks after Wilson's second Inaugural in 1917, he and his Administration—the White House, that is—became the overlord of the United States in a manner no President had been before. The accumulation of authority was so swift—power that was transferred from the Congress to the White House—that nothing subsequently has stripped much of it from the Executive arm of the Government.

Its image grew even larger during the fighting period by the sheer weight of the names of men who acted as its deputies—Daniel Willard running the national rail-

The lights burned late at night during these critical times

roads, Bernard M. Baruch as the czar of munitions production, Herbert Clark Hoover oragnizing conservation of the nation's food supplies, Julius Rosenwald coordinating all clothing production.

At the thunderous climax of victory in Europe, Wilson received the full credit for mobilizing the country for the war, and then set out in a new role for an American President—that of an equal among world leaders to write the peace. But, although it was not recognized immediately, the dream was dead, killed in the indirect manner of American elections. The same Americans who, through their elected Congressmen, had given the White House almost supreme authority to wage a war, drew back from such a vote of confidence when confronted with the waging of peace. In November 1918, when the Armistice was signed, the electorate a few days earlier had already overthrown the Democratic majorities in both the Senate and the House.

Before that election the leadership of the White House seemingly was unquestioned in world councils; after that election the European Allies got down to business on the old basis of balance of power. At home the voters repudiated *147* centralized control of the United States and strengthened the hands of the isolationists.

To make all the controversy more tearing in terms of White House prestige, Wilson created an enormous precedent in December 1918 by sailing to Europe to head his own mission to the Versailles Peace Conference. He was the first President in office to set foot on foreign soil, and he returned there in 1919, finally helping to write a treaty of 85,000 words, including a charter for the League of Nations.

The defeat of that treaty is now part of the past, but its sequel—the illness of Wilson—still echos in the 1960s. A pending amendment to the Constitution, passed by the Congress and submitted to the States in 1966, attempts to define steps to be taken in the case of the disability of a President. Debates still echoed from the days when Mrs. Edith Wilson indirectly controlled the White House as a wife sheltering her invalid husband.

The circumstances were so extraordinary during the last days of the Wilson Administration—and almost unbelievable less than fifty years later—that perhaps a brief account will help to clarify them.

By the 1960s the White House has become a vast machinery run by a large secretariat and special assistants to the President who virtually rank with the Cabinet in their assignments to various areas of Government activity. One of these has the sole duty of maintaining daily contact with Congressional leaders of both parties. Instant communication between the President and all parts of the Executive establishment is available, even when he is riding in an automobile or an airplane. In matters of vital interest, he can summon television facilities to talk to the entire nation on an hour's notice.

Yet in the second decade of this century, despite the strengthening of government in World War I, Wilson acted as Chief Executive, advised by a Cabinet from whose members he remained strangely aloof except for formal sessions. He had a single secretary, Joseph Tumulty. He abhorred the telephone and communicated with others by handwritten notes, carried around by elderly messengers. His only contact with Congress was direct and personal through the summoning of selected members for leisurely talks. One operator sufficed to man the White House switchboard, and one telegraph operator handled other communications by wire. The clerical staff was small. Travel was only by train or by automobile, and involved a slow and ponderous movement handled by the Secret Service.

In all ordinary affairs the White House was a large and impressive private house, with a small office wing. It was set in the same park-like surroundings that tourists see today, but its rooms, except for formal occasions, were largely unoccupied. Early in his Administration, Wilson made it clear that he considered the White House so private to him and his family that he threatened to horsewhip any news reporter who presumed to report unauthorized news about his family.

In most respects Wilson lived behind a psychological moat which he early dug around the White House. This was later intensified by the war and treaty crises, but it was due also to the circumstances

President Wilson arrives at the White House

of his second marriage.

Many observers who knew Wilson well —and he had a certain charm—commented afterward that he had brought to the White House an unparalleled idealism, but that an obtuse streak of vanity that had turned political contests into matters of personal contention wrecked him and probably caused his premature death. This finally involved Mrs. Edith Galt Wilson in an impossible situation, which recalled the biting gossip that had occurred in 1915 when, within a year of his first wife's death, Wilson married the mature Washington widow.

When Wilson made his second return from Europe in 1919 with the 85,000-word treaty providing for the League of Nations, he invited the Foreign Relations Committee of the Senate to the White House for a long discussion of it. The Committee studied the proposal, which would have to be ratified by the Senate, and attached to it thirty-eight amendments and four reservations.

Angered, Wilson was said to have de- 149

manded ratification of "his" treaty without the crossing of a *t* or the dotting of an *i*. He seemed to forget that as a politician he had no majority support in the Senate, or that he was not dealing with a class of college undergraduates, but with men of long experience and rare talents in politics. The chairman of the committee was the first Senator Henry Cabot Lodge, a scholarly conservative from Massachusetts. Two of the more vocal and brilliantly oratorical Republican members were Hiram Johnson of California and William Edgar Borah of Idaho, both liberals. But all joined in anger at Wilson's dictum. Wilson had the support of former President Taft, of Herbert Hoover and many other notable Republicans, but they were not in the Senate.

Immediately after the Foreign Relations Committee made its qualified report on the treaty, Wilson set out to barnstorm the country in support of it. On September 21 he collapsed in Pueblo, Colorado, and was carried back to a hushed house where not only were the doors locked but the gates in the fences surrounding the lawns as well.

The White House became its own ghost, while the machinery of government plowed through demobilization. Tumulty complained that he could only see the President, as the latter made a slow partial recovery, at Mrs. Wilson's behest and in her presence. Secretary of State Lansing finally called a meeting of the Cabinet, but was reprimanded for it by Wilson.

In some instances, it was reported, Mrs. Wilson would transmit verbal messages from the President, while the paralyzed man sat helplessly in his chair and was occasionally entertained with movies contributed by the producing companies. But never once did Wilson offer either to resign or to delegate authority.

His friends did all they could to protect him, and it is a notable sidelight that—aside from the treaty contention—no elements of the opposition ever attempted to overthrow him or the office as he occupied it.

When his term expired the President left the White House, to move into a private mansion in Washington which, it was learned almost fifty years later, was more expensive than his small fortune could afford and represented in part a gift from wealthy friends, including some Republicans.

There was a flurry in 1920, the election year of that quadrennium, when a number of Democrats were hoping against hope to select a candidate who might win. Among those who searched for a candidate was the youthful Assistant Secretary of the Navy, who was rounding out eight years in the Wilson "little Cabinet." His name was Franklin Delano Roosevelt. Among those he called upon to sound out as a possible Presidential candidate was a distinguished individual with no avowed political connections. Thus an offer of support for the Democratic nomination was made to Herbert Hoover, who turned it down.

Instead, the Democratic Convention nominated Governor James M. Cox, of Ohio, who went down to stunning defeat; defeated with him was the Vice Presidential nominee, Roosevelt.

The Green Room during the Harding Administration

After the formalities of the election in 1920, it seemed for a while that the White House had been permanently shorn of much of the prestige and authority painstakingly built into its modern development by Theodore Roosevelt, and, prior to 1919, by Wilson.

Even the slogans of the political season seemed to gloat over this change. A Republican Convention had nominated Warren G. Harding, Senate majority leader and handsome, eloquent speech-maker, after adopting a platform denouncing "executive autocracy." And Harding adopted for his campaign slogan the words, "Back to Normalcy."

In historical perspective, this might have been considered a normal turn of the political wheel, but changes of Administration are not made for history. This was a hard, vicious fight to strip the President of much of his authority and to substitute a form of Congressional "leadership" for the Executive authority.

In living memory Harding was the weakest man ever put into position to win the Presidency. It seemed that the Republican leadership which picked him as the White House "front man" reached even further in the field of weak candidates for the nation's highest office to nominate Calvin Coolidge for the Vice Presidency. Coolidge could not even hold his audiences when he went campaigning.

Now, in the cold hindsight of years long past, it seems that the White House survived Harding—although with rumpled prestige—because he lived only two years and a few months in that office. Then Coolidge picked up the pieces and slowly restored the dignity of the mansion, while Mrs. Grace Coolidge exhibited a rare knack for assisting in this work.

The architects of the Harding Administration have ceased to be important, but they put together a Cabinet for him that included some names which have grown in reputation over the years and others who precipitated the Teapot Dome oil scandal and other shenanigans comparable only with the ring of men who tried to corner the gold market under President Grant. As for Harding's role, it has been agreed that he was never personally dishonest; he was simply stupid.

The great minds who helped to buttress the White House as an institution and to save its reputation were Hoover, who became and remained Secretary of Commerce for twelve years; Charles Evans Hughes as Secretary of State, who eventually resigned to become Chief Justice of the United States; A. W. Mellon as Secretary of the Treasury who contributed and gathered the original collection for the National Gallery of Art; and Henry C. Wallace, the first Secretary of Agriculture.

When the public spoke of the White House in these early years they usually meant the personalities around the President, rather than the figurehead of government.

Harding's habits that bred unpopularity —mostly of a sort not connected with official life—were causing a bad reaction by 1923. It was decided that he should travel and, by displaying his talents in personal appearances, help to repair the damage. A journey by train across the United States and a voyage to Alaska were scheduled for the summer.

Harding went to Alaska, and returned

The State Dining Room

to resume the train tour. However, since he seemed tired from the journey, his train was halted in San Francisco for an added rest period. There on the night of August 2, 1923, Harding died.

If there was anything that the White House seemed to need politically and socially at this point in its development, it was material for a homely legend—dry humor, personal anecdotes, and homespun character to wash away the memories of war and profiteering, official scandals and overpolished oratory.

Coolidge, as though provided with props, rehearsal notes, and makeup, was waiting in the wings. If it is necessary to emphasize how far out of the picture Vice Presidents were even in 1923 (unless the President died), it may be recalled that Coolidge was vacationing in his father's house in Plymouth, Massachusetts, so

President Harding and Madame Marie Curie in the South Grounds

remote from a telephone that five hours were required to install one for him by hastily running a wire from an adjoining town. Kerosene lamps lighted the living room of this house, while his father, a justice of the peace, administered to him the oath of his new office.

The hour in history had arrived when a President who could do virtually nothing, could keep his mouth shut, and give a good appearance of sincere concern for the country could become useful. Coolidge did. And thus he rebuilt the dignity of the White House and gave it a new and solid personality.

Coolidge seemed to encourage stories about himself, as long as they did not demean his office. When he moved into the White House, he and Mrs. Coolidge soon established a reputation for tasteful and luxurious entertaining. The opulent refurnishings of 1902 had become soiled and frayed, and money was appropriated

for their repair and replacement, which Mrs. Coolidge superintended with deliberate attempt to replace—not change—whatever was needed.

Then a survey of the building made by the Army Corps of Engineers revealed that the roof beams were rotted and that a new roof would have to be installed. Thus, in historical progression, while the roof was being replaced, it was raised and a new bedroom floor with eight additional rooms was added to the original building.

President Coolidge gave the appearance of a man who always wore the same suit, but after he became President he made a point of being tailored by the best cutters, and he had a large wardrobe; nonetheless, all the suits looked the same. He had a hound dog's nose for smelling out waste in government (as in the case of the White House food bills), but he used the old and costly *Mayflower* for

154

weekends far more than other Presidents —particularly since he disliked traveling as much as he hated spending unnecessary time in the White House.

In the operation of the White House, Coolidge accepted customs already established, but he lost one notable campaign for economy—a fight involving his travel expenses, for the sake of the Government, not for himself.

Looking back in a day of jet aircraft and fleets of helicopters always at the disposal of the White House, it may seem a little ridiculous to talk about Presidential railroad charges, but this recollection is not told lightly.

Up to the time of the Taft Administration, the great American symbol of prestige was the railroad pass. Officials were carried free, and, for that matter, so was almost everyone from business or the professions. Naturally the courtesy was extended to Presidents, members of Congress and the Washington hierarchy. Then a "reform wave" swept through Congress and it provided specified travel allowances for various officials and strictly forbade railroads to issue any passes whatsoever—a rule that still holds. For the President, an annual travel allowance of $25,000 was appropriated.

This is a fairly generous figure, particularly as the President pays only for his personal party, while the Treasury Department pays expenses of the Secret Service, and newspapers and broadcasting companies pay the expenses of their correspondents, photographers, and technicians. But the rub was that when the President traveled he took, and was expected to take, a private car, which cost much more than the fares paid individually by those who accompanied him.

For a vacation trip to the Black Hills, Coolidge determined that this would be a foolish expense. He ordered accommodations for himself in a regular drawing room. This was a newsworthy gesture, but it upset the various affected railroads, which had established a safety record for never having lost or injured a Presidential passenger.

Maybe Coolidge knew—and it would have been strange for him not to know—that the Presidential trains were set aside from normal schedules, that tracks were cleared ahead of them and tested by a pilot train run ahead, that all cars which were parked on adjoining tracks were removed while the special train passed. In desperation the railroads simply ran the President's train on which he had the drawing room as a special train.

Before the President took another trip, the Interstate Commerce Commission had ruled that the Secret Service might order into service any equipment necessary to insure the President's safety. Thereafter, the old special trains were back in duty. The President's travel allowance, which he could not pocket in any event, showed a nice surplus, and this ruling later permitted Franklin D. Roosevelt to travel a record 200,000 miles by train in his first two terms without straining a budget that remained at the same size.

Dignity, not glamour, was Mrs. Coolidge's *forte* as First Lady. In passing, it may be noted that she was the first college graduate to become mistress of the White House, as distinguished from some earlier wives who had attended junior seminaries

President Harding's coffin lies in the East Room

Movie star Tom Mix pays a visit to the White House; President Coolidge looks on

then termed "colleges." While presiding over her regular duties, Mrs. Coolidge found time to knit the President's socks, and to crochet in two years a bedspread for the Lincoln bed.

In that atmosphere the "Coolidge era" went onto a quiet shelf of White House history, beginning and ending in prosperity and seemingly settled into a quiet groove forever.

When Herbert Hoover was elected to succeed Coolidge his image was that of a conservative, reliable custodian for a rich and contented country that had rounded out its frontiers and established its destiny.

There had never been a President like Hoover, or a First Lady even remotely like his wife, Lou Henry Hoover. He was a self-made man from the days of his Quaker boyhood in Iowa. By the time he graduated as an engineer from Leland Stanford University, in California, he and his bride-to-be had become internationally famous in select circles for their translation of *De Re Metallica,* a work on mining from the Middle Ages written in Latin by Agricola.

Caught in Peking by the Boxer Rebelion, Hoover helped to prepare the defenses for the besieged foreign colony. Soon afterward he was in Russia, surveying mineral resources for that government. Long before World War I the taciturn engineer headed his world-wide engineering firm, lived magnificently in London, and was able and willing to drop all his private interests to administer Belgian relief after World War I began. When he became Secretary of Commerce in 1920 he bought a luxurious Washington mansion, settled down to devote the rest of his

President and Mrs. Hoover sponsor an egg-roll and Maypole dance on the White House lawn at Easter

life to public service, and showed a total disinterest in politics. No one ever knew the extent of his wealth, but from the start as Secretary of Commerce he arranged to endorse his own salary check over to his secretary as the latter's salary.

Famed and almost revered when he died in 1965, as a forward-looking scholar of government, Hoover experienced in the White House a deep chasm separating his earlier glamorous career and his subsequent appreciation as an elder statesman. It has been said on more than one occasion that Hoover would have had a greater place in history had he not had the bad luck to be elected President in his time, or had he not in choosing a political affiliation joined the Republican Party at one of its most conservative periods.

The author considers this judgment ridiculous. The White House gives no aspirant, successful or other, a choice in these matters. Who has ever eschewed a trial at the Presidency? How many men in later years have wished it all might have been different?

The Presidency is a force in government, but it also is subject to circumstance; Congress, being too large and cross-hatched with regional and other interests, being unable to exert leadership, too often hurls new authority at the White House when it panics, and then makes the White House a scapegoat when things go wrong.

In October 1929, just six months after Hoover's first and only Inaugural, things went wrong indeed. The panic that hit the Stock Exchange ballooned into the Depression, which would continue with small variation for years.

15 Turn of the Wheel

Franklin D. Roosevelt entered the White House with a promise to give a "new deal" to the American people.

The time and the circumstance and the personality were right for turning the New Deal into a revolutionary movement that changed the meaning and character of the White House as never before in periods of transition. The early history ended with Herbert Hoover; the new history ever

The East Room during FDR's Administration

since Inaugural Day in 1933 has been an onrushing one of change not even halted, let alone checked by the period in which the Republican Party recaptured control.

And it should be noted here with emphasis that among the aging patriots no one worked harder for progress in the later years than Herbert Hoover.

To a degree hard at first to realize—above the bickerings and political debate that normally arose in the later Roosevelt years—there came about a change in the character of the White House that has been compared in some respects to the change that occurred with Andrew Jackson's occupancy.

Jackson was elected President by a smaller but vigorous country that rebelled against the conservatism marking the Presidency from the beginning of the Republic through John Quincy Adams. Even Jefferson's radicalism, for his time, rapidly blended into the traditions of the old South, of old New England, and the equally old intermediate patterns of life and thought of the eastern seacoast.

The West of Jackson's time did not necessarily have better ideas, or a better voice, but it demanded to be heard. Above all, it wanted change.

It was and has continued to be fortunate that the liberal revolutions swirling around the White House all have been fought out at the polls, not by mobs or armed forces. (Yes, there was the Civil War, but that essentially was a contest by conservatives to maintain the status quo.) It continues to be a surprising fact that among the major powers of the world the United States is the oldest country in the world with a basically unchanged form of government. The three great symbols of that fact are the White House, the Capitol, and the Supreme Court. It might be said that in this triumvirate of government the White House proposes, the Capitol disposes, and the Supreme Court sits over both as the watchdog and guardian of the people's interests.

Nevertheless, the mood of the country focuses only in one reflection, the White House itself, and the "tone" which that establishment radiates. This grew very dull indeed during the Hoover Administration. Even the city seemed to feel a little ashamed of itself, as though it were trying to hide from the spotlight. It was more drab as a setting for the White House than actually needed to be the case.

The diplomats on generous allowances from their home governments, the very wealthy on fixed incomes and the government employees had, in the period of declining prices, often higher purchasing power than before the Depression. But spending became less conspicuous. One by one the palatial houses were closed while their owners moved—often into equally fine ones—into less conspicuous regions in the suburbs. When the unemployed veterans who were termed the "bonus marchers" started to squat in vacant buildings, the Washington atmosphere became even more tense.

Public buildings grew dingy, even the gardening was neglected in the parks, and, instead of visitors flocking to Washington to help spark the social life, the trend was reversed and Washingtonians found more excuses to visit elsewhere.

The Hoovers maintained the social formalities of the White House, but the President, in the half year of mild weather, spent more and more time at a fishing cottage he had established on the Rapidan River in Virginia.

In fairness to Herbert Hoover, it should be noted that when he might have drawn on his experience to do the most, he never had a chance. The Congress which in the early days of the Depression backed his hand in a first tentative effort to make loans for relief purposes to the States finally backed away from such "radical" legislation when the cost mounted.

The great change that came to the White House in 1933 was not alone in the character of the new President, but in the fact that his associates were politically new. It was time for a change of leadership, a change of pace, even though on careful examination there was much less that was new about the personalities involved than a romantic description would indicate.

F. D. Roosevelt was an old Washington hand. With the aid of their private means Mr. and Mrs. Roosevelt had lived in rare elegance compared to other official families who had only their salaries to support them. The top half of the Roosevelt Cabinet, headed by Secretary of State Cordell Hull, were very experienced Washington types.

Among the new faces were a handful including the Brain Trust who had been built up by advance publicity into a sort of mystery group.

Aside from all this detail, the important development that made the White House suddenly interesting and vital to public interest was Roosevelt's own personality. He gave both his friends and his enemies

something to talk about. He put life into the White House. He had lengthy engagement lists. He flooded the Congress with measures dealing with the recovery program. He took dramatic steps, as in the employment relief and public works program, and in a country not yet accustomed to thinking in large sums of money he borrowed and spent billions on these projects.

The White House assumed a leadership never developed in peacetime, and it became a personality with a voice when Roosevelt introduced the "fireside chats," given almost weekly in his first few months in office to "my friends."

Meanwhile, within the White House, a political skill sometimes comparable with the President's own was at work in the person of Mrs. Roosevelt.

At first announcing that formal social affairs would be held to a minimum, she soon turned the routine into an active one that might seem less formal but was never dull. Officials had their proper turns in entertaining and being entertained, but Mrs. Roosevelt added others—youth groups, organizations, and people of interest—to the invitation lists. It was not long before thousands of persons, leaders from all walks of life, had been entertained in a manner which had been reserved for the very select few.

Of course, there were the critics, who grew more and more vocal about the changes made by the Roosevelts—criticism that always accompanies radical change, and that was given possibly more than the usual foundation by the extreme individuality of the five Roosevelt children. Four of these piled up a formidable list of cumulative marriages, divorces, and children—principally in the period of their father's Presidency. The fifth, John, a schoolboy when F.D.R. was elected, became the single conservative in the family.

Finally when Mrs. Roosevelt added to her long-established lecture tours the writing of a daily news column and of magazine articles for publication, the cup of criticism—from all those looking for something to criticize—ran over.

Roosevelt's aura of newness survived, but barely, his first term, but his re-election for a second with victory in all but two States had made his personality synonymous with the personality of the White House.

It had become a center of violent controversy, but it was no longer drab; its brightly lighted windows and grounds seemed to reflect back some of the cheerier attitude of a country that was fighting its way out of the Depression.

What happened inevitably in the peacetime era of the Roosevelt Administrations was a definite, if indefinable, change in the status of the White House. In earlier generations it had stood periodically as a symbol of leadership, only to drift back in successive waves into a lackluster residence of the Presidents.

By 1937, when the first steps toward recovery had achieved some of their purpose, there came a test that proved the difference between this most recent ascendancy and other periods that had marked declines. Roosevelt overreached himself in trying to force through Congress legislation to change the terms and conditions of Supreme Court membership, in order to retire some older conservatives and put more of his own "liberals" on the bench. He lost that fight, when his own

Congressional leadership turned against him.

But an important aspect of this defeat was that it hardly dented and certainly did not diminish the prestige of the White House as an institution. It continued to be the house of "the Chief," a seat of power and of leadership. The White House had never risen so high in all its peacetime history. Only war leadership could elevate its stature, and in 1939, before Roosevelt's second term had run its course, war had started in Europe.

Incidentally, that expression, "war had started in Europe," itself shows the contradictory effect that comes from attempting to compartmentalize eras in the White House or any government into tidy little cubicles. The correct expression would be that hostilities had begun in Europe, because we now see that World War II was merely an extension of unsolved difficulties left over from World War I, just as many of the problems, tensions, and fighting today represent the unfinished business of World War II.

The first action by Roosevelt after his Inaugural in 1933 is a dramatic example of the always-growing powers of the White House, generally born in emergencies but remaining as additions to authority or as precedents.

Roosevelt's first act as a new President was to close the banks and otherwise start to clamp controls on money, to stem the public panic. He took this action under a law called the *Trading with the Enemy Act,* hastily passed by Congress in 1917, to which was attached one amendment that would be applied to the banking emergency sixteen years later.

161

In the New Deal period, also, the White House became a much greater seat of power by indirect means, the operation of which became clear only with the passage of time. Under the cloak of the appropriations for public works, Roosevelt started a sizable building program for the Navy, without rousing pacifist objections by requesting funds specifically for that purpose. As an Executive action he "traded" Britain a fleet of destroyers for Navy bases in the Western Atlantic without seeking advance approval from Congress.

Roosevelt multiplied the assumption of powers, but now students are learning more and more that the powers were always there; they were only waiting to be used.

In earlier days Calvin Coolidge—who sometimes broke his taciturnity with some really philosophical observations—remarked to an older friend of the writer, who had known him well: "The only reason a tyrant has never ruled in the White House is that we have always chosen Presidents who did not want to be tyrants."

Roosevelt never became a "tyrant," or a dictator, but in his long tenure he came to personify a new kind of White House and a new White House power. The voice of government was the voice of the White House, the leadership of government rested in the White House, and when war came, the command was in the White House. This was due partly to circumstances and partly to the personality of the President, but it gave an unshakable new dignity and size to the White House.

After Pearl Harbor, no other leadership in government existed except that grouped under the White House symbol. In fact,

before that time in the so-called "emergency period," Roosevelt used the White House symbolism to form the first real coalition government in American history. This completely took the wind out of the sails of any possible future attempt to form a strong opposition in the Congress. Two of the leading names in the Republican Party joined his Cabinet, and just below them were a host of prominent persons who normally would have been among his critical opponents.

Henry L. Stimson, one of New York's most prominent Republicans, a lawyer and former Secretary of State, answered an appeal to his patriotism and became Roosevelt's Secretary of War (this was before there was a Defense Department). At the same time Frank Knox, Chicago publisher and once a candidate for the Vice Presidency on the Republican ticket, became Secretary of the Navy.

Robert Patterson, another noted New York lawyer and Republican, became Stimson's Undersecretary of War, and James V. Forrestal, the financier, became Assistant Secretary of the Navy, a stepping stone that eventually led him to be the first Secretary of Defense.

Wilson had placed men of relatively equal prominence in the group advising the White House and administering programs in World War I; Roosevelt gave these Republicans seats of authority on policy in World War II.

And it was highly significant that in 1944, with the second great war still awaiting an indeterminate end, Roosevelt reached into the Senate to choose for his Vice President Harry S Truman, who had built up a solidly conservative reputation as chairman of the very special "watch-dog" committee for that body on the conduct of the war.

As the White House grew as an institution, with its increased responsibilities of war leadership, it changed little in appearance, although considerably in its functional spaces. Long before the outbreak of war, the offices became so inadequate that another addition was made to the west office wing, but with such skill that passersby hardly noticed the difference.

An equally deceptive addition was made under the east wing, partly by excavation and partly by extension back into the garden, with construction of a presumably bombproof suite of offices termed the "map room," but in effect the supreme headquarters of the war offices—presided over by Fleet Admiral William Leahy, the President's Chief of Staff, and served by communications covering the world.

Within the White House the accommodations for visitors were again strained to the limit, under the historic rule that chiefs of state and major heads of government had to be entertained at least briefly as "house guests."

Among these there were the usual callers of the first rank who under all circumstances would sleep in the White House, such as Winston Churchill (enthusiastically received.) and Charles de Gaulle.

But the guest list of members of royal families and smaller governments-in-exile, mostly crowding official quarters in or near London, soon began arriving in Washington. They were welcomed for whatever encouragement a show of American friendship gave to their own

A press conference, FDR style

One of FDR's famous Fireside Chats

people in occupied countries. Before the war ended, a visit to Washington was considered obligatory by the exiles for postwar value when they returned to their homelands.

Protocol was changed historically when the Government purchased Blair House—the same residence occupied by the former advisers of Jackson and Lincoln—across Pennsylvania Avenue from the White House as a sort of bedroom annex for these official guests. This house also gave the Secretary of State an entertainment house, although not a residence, where he could give his own interminable but necessary dinners and receptions.

In the progression of such moves, Blair House soon became inadequate for its purposes, and an adjoining old mansion, named Blair-Lee House, was added to it.

All of these changes and additions indicated the great changes in the spirit of the White House, but there was one major development that in retrospect had a growing importance. That was the revolutionary development in communications wrought by the war.

In effect, the President and his staff came into almost immediate contact at will with the military forces deployed around the world. The former delays in communications caused by weather or limited land facilities were overcome by improvements in radio transmissions. Machines were perfected with capabilities of almost instantaneous coding and decoding of messages. Larger and faster airplanes carried the couriers with their pouches on most confidential errands.

164   The upshot of this was that the Presi-

dent and his staff, even in the later phases of his overseas travel, were in instant touch with the war and with the Allied governments. And this meant that only the President was so advised from all quarters.

Unlike Lincoln, who sat wrapped in a blanket alongside a telegraph operator in the War Department waiting for news from his generals, the President was constantly informed from six continents.

Yet in thus picturing the fantastic changes made by war in the old White House, there is one anecdote that illustrates how the past always drags along to supply some gap still existing in the present.

After Pearl Harbor there was, for a time, a very real fear that German ingenuity might find some way to mount air raids on leading cities of the eastern seacoast, and on Washington in particular. No one knew that this could be done, but then neither had anyone believed the devastating Japanese attack on Pearl Harbor was possible.

Washington was prepared for defense against eventual attack by air, with the mounting of antiaircraft guns in suburban emplacements, on the roofs of some buildings such as the Treasury Department, and in the parks.

One of the larger guns was emplaced a short distance from the wall of the White House adjacent to the south gardens. It was very effective as a visible defense weapon that could be seen by passersby. The gun had a five-inch bore—the largest of its type, and it reached very high into the air. It was manned by crews who

The major structural change in the mansion during Roosevelt's four Administrations was the addition of a swimming pool

vigorously rehearsed the actions of handling the gun.

One day Major General Edwin M. Watson, Roosevelt's military aide and long-time White House intimate, stopped and surveyed the gun, looking with an experienced eye at it, at the White House, and the ammunition piled nearby. When he returned to the White House offices, he remarked, "Better take the ammunition away from that gun out there. If some joker ever fires one of those shells, you may as well tell Hitler not to bother trying to bomb us. The concussion would bring down the whole house."

Roosevelt died—not in the White House, but in Warm Springs, Georgia—on April 12, 1945. He left the White House beyond doubt the most powerful center in any free nation, with an unprecedented combination of wartime authority exercisable under the President's "emergency powers."

We can only guess what the story would have been had the same man with the same accumulated powers served out the almost full term of office that lay before him.

Scaffolding supports the sagging ceiling of the East Room

The new electric kitchen being installed

The new concrete being poured to support the ground floor

A workman scrubs the marble floor of the first-floor main hall

President Truman rehearses a speech in his White House office

Covering the walls of the President's study with cloth

Harry S Truman had every opportunity to make as much of a mess of his succession to the White House as had Andrew Johnson. It is to the credit of his personality and the maturity of the institution that he went on to win re-election in his own right, and to grow in the public's respect and affection.

The news of Roosevelt's death—at the close of a busy and apparently healthy morning at Warm Springs, Georgia, while he was resting in his secluded cottage—came as a shocking surprise to the world, and most of all to Truman, who had been following a quiet Vice President's routine and living unostentatiously with his family in a Washington apartment.

Within a few hours Truman was hustled to temporary living quarters in Blair House, not for the sake of dignity but so that the Secret Service could protect him better. And his initiation into the intricate world of war and international politics began. The White House claimed its new master before he had a chance to assert his own claim, or before he knew much more about the new empire he had inherited than do most readers of the daily newspapers.

Out of the Truman experiences, and the deep concern over what might have been, grew changes in the status of Vice Presidents and other concern over the assurance of more orderly succession to the White House in possible future emergencies of this nature. This warrants a word of explanation.

As Vice President, Truman was an ex-

A carved wooden replica of the Presidential Seal is added to the East Room doorway

He entered office as the dependent and hostage of the military leadership. Credit for his rapid tutelage is given to Admiral Leahy and to General George C. Marshall, the pinnacles of power for the Navy and Army. Fortunately neither possessed any ambition or jealousy beyond serving his country and his new President. The same was true of the other leaders who contributed to the miracle whereby within weeks the new President could intelligently and skillfully step into leadership of the conference for founding the United Nations at San Francisco, travel abroad to confer with his co-leaders of national forces on the eve of victory in Europe, and assume the terrible responsibility of unleashing the atom bomb on Japan.

This is not a critique analyzing how well Truman did his job. It is amazing that he—or anyone else for that matter—could do it at all. He enlarged the White House stature while maturing his own political personality. He was a principal architect of the post-World War II world, enlarged radically the peacetime effectiveness of the White House leadership and, in passing, reconstructed the edifice itself.

Serving as President in a spot bracketed between Roosevelt and Dwight D. Eisenhower, Truman brought to the White House some of the rural and homespun flavor of older Presidents with a frontier background. He shared some of their predilection for loyalties to former political associates who were cold, practical politicians, as well as their unexpected appreciation—as in the case of Jackson—for the essential dignity of the mansion and the office it exemplified.

perienced politician and had recently come into this office from distinguished service in the Senate. He was intimately in touch with studies of the American participation, but he also shared the ignorance of even the senior average members of Congress about high strategy and plans.

Except for a formal handshake, Truman had never visited with Winston Churchill or even met Stalin or other Allied leaders. It has been reported that he did not even know the secret of development of the atom bomb, or how close it was to becoming a reality.

168

A remarkable tribute was paid to Truman's contribution to White House development of prestige, in his later years, when veteran Washington observers began to describe him as an outstanding authority on American traditions and history. His formal schooling had ended with high school in Lamar, Missouri, where he was born. His world contact had begun and ended with overseas service in World War I. Prior to his Senate service, his highest distinction had been that of a county judge in Missouri—a post possible for a non-lawyer, to which Truman was appointed, and after which he took law courses in Kansas City.

Yet his actions—or those of his advisers acting in the name of the White House—gave to history most of the twentieth-century deeds denoting America's world leadership. Among them were the Marshall Plan, ECA, rehabilitation of Greece and Turkey, establishment of NATO and naming of Eisenhower as its first Supreme Commander, leadership in UN opposition to the Communist invasion of South Korea and eventual dismissal of General Douglas MacArthur for disagreeing with Truman's policies. Incidentally, while asserting White House absolute control over even the most prominent military commanders, Truman set Eisenhower on the path to succeed him and finally gave one of his heartiest evidences of support to General Marshall as his Secretary of State.

It is now time to turn to the imprint which Truman left upon the building itself and which, despite recent embellishments, promises to remain at least as long

Workman in front of the two magnolias originally planted by Andrew Jackson

as the Theodore Roosevelt alteration did.

Truman was during all his public life a gregarious and vigorous man, who was already sixty years old, only two years junior to Roosevelt, when he succeeded him to the Presidency. Mrs. Truman was a year younger, and their one child Margaret was in 1945 only twenty-one.

When the Trumans entered the White House, it soon became evident that for them it was simply an extension of political life, perhaps surrounded by many new luxuries that they felt no inclination to change. To it they would not subordinate their own established patterns, including

169

A moving van arrives at Blair House. The Trumans spent nearly half of their White House years in Blair House, while the Presidential mansion was being rebuilt.

continued usage of their modest home in Independence, Missouri, which over the years they had modernized and personalized. Margaret Truman continued her studies and musical practice that led eventually to a brief career as a concert and broadcast singer—all of which made the usual headlines.

Then it began to dawn on the public that the new President possessed an informality that he preserved at all costs.

In the East Room of the White House is a concert grand piano, presented by the Steinway Piano Company in the 1902 reconstruction. Many great concert artists, including Paderewski, have used it in formal engagements. Harry Truman also played it, at informal parties, and on one occasion permitted a photograph to be made of a leggy popular singer sitting on top of the piano while he accompanied her on the keyboard. Popular artists were welcomed at White House parties, not as

"command performers" but as guests, and Margaret matured among them.

Harry Truman liked colorful sports shirts to such an extent that some haberdashers still refer to the loud ones as "Truman shirts," and while he dressed conservatively on formal occasions, photographers delighted in taking pictures of him wearing his new ones on holidays.

Furthermore, Truman liked—and still likes, so far as is known—to take long walks. (So did Teddy Roosevelt, but his walks were usually hikes in the woods, as on one occasion he was reported to have taken Jules Jusserand, French Ambassador for a stroll in the wild part of Rock Creek Park while studiously overlooking the Ambassador's costume of frock coat and top hat donned for a formal White House call.) In Truman's more than twenty years in and out of the White House he may be credited with having improved the health—or in some cases

The new solarium on the top floor of the White House

with having ruined the health—of countless news correspondents, because his favorite walking hour was about 6 A.M,. and he welcomed the press accompaniment. During his walks he gave out some of his most important remarks and he was always his most charming. Of course, he also was accompanied by a Secret Service escort, but these men worked on shifts around the clock.

And it was Truman, often violently criticized as a "politician" in the White House in the conduct of domestic affairs, who set two precedents for the office— both dealing with the opposition—that certainly will be cited in the future for the guidance of Presidents to come.

First, there was the case of Herbert Hoover, who was so ostracized by Franklin D. Roosevelt that it has been said he never visited Washington (and certainly was not officially entertained in the White House) from 1933 to 1945. In 1947 Tru-

man invited Hoover to accept the post of Coordinator of the European Food Program. Later in that same year he named Hoover as chairman of the Commission for Reorganization of the Executive Branch.

A few years later, when Eisenhower was President and was having extreme difficulties with Congress in trying to put a legislative program into shape against the combined opposition of Republicans and Democrats, Truman snapped out in a public statement: "Our government cannot function properly unless the President is master in his own house."

By the time of Truman's Administrations the White House had become so overloaded with traditions and alterations that one morning the President noted his bathtub was beginning to settle into the floor. This was in 1948, and it posed a serious problem, because only a year 171 earlier Truman had been embroiled in nation-wide debate over the only, and a minor, change he had made in the mansion. In that year he had ordered construction of a gallery, high up under the circular south portico, with access from the family quarters. It was immediately dubbed the "front porch," and traditionalists made it a national issue.

By any standards the White House was very old, and the limestone used for its foundations and walls as an economy measure long since has been required to carry burdens never dreamed of by Hoban: added floors, heavier roofs, and all the modern improvements such as plumbing, heating, and electric wiring.

As in Coolidge's era, there was the suggestion that the building be abandoned as a residence and simply restored for use as a museum. That suggestion was immediately vetoed. The second suggestion was that the White House be rebuilt from the ground up, all new, in replica of the original.

Finally, in consultations with engineers and architects, Truman gave the ultimate decision that the White House must remain as the public knew it, and that the repairs must be made from inside out. Despite, the higher cost, which was $5,761,000, as compared with tearing down the exterior and starting afresh, Congress enthusiastically approved.

The interior was gutted, but so carefully that all mantels, lighting fixtures, pieces of metal ornamental work, paneling, and plaster moldings were numbered and stored. Then work was undertaken that would not have been possible with the machinery and equipment in Theodore Roosevelt's time.

New underpinning extending downward for twenty-four feet was placed under the outside walls to prevent their sinking or going out of plumb in the future. Inside these walls was erected a steel frame standing independently of the old masonry, and within which were placed the new beams and other structural members. Over these went the restored interior walls, ceilings, and other details of the house.

The job took four years, ending in 1952. In that period the Truman family lived across the street in Blair House.

Here on November 1, 1950, two Puerto Rican fanatics attempted to storm the building and assassinate the President. They were stopped by guards, but at the cost of one guard's life and the wounding of two others, while an amazed President watched the brief engagement from a second-floor window.

The supreme Army commanders in three major wars fought by the United States have established a tradition that victory leads to the Presidency. They are Washington, Grant, and Eisenhower. In Eisenhower's case it took a little longer, but it seems in retrospect that Eisenhower won election and re-election as a civilian and not in any sense as a military conqueror.

Yet it was as a disciplined military product that the Allied Supreme Commander in Europe conducted the Presidency; and, after his terms, he retired like Cincinnatus to his quiet farm. The exception to the comparison came only after he was out of office and when he fought to reframe the Republican Party to his liking.

Eisenhower's role in the pages of the White House story is an extraordinary one that already has become confused in his own lifetime. It is as unique as that of Truman, but with entirely different overtones and byplays.

While Eisenhower is six years younger than Truman, both started as farm boys in the Middle West, and after graduation from local schools both tried for appointments to West Point. One won admission; the other, Truman, failed to pass the eye tests. In World War I, the civilian Truman went overseas with a National Guard unit and ended the war as a major. At that point Eisenhower had become a lieutenant colonel in command of a tank corps, but during that war he remained in the United States.

Truman first won his Senate seat in 1934, while Eisenhower was serving on staff duty in Washington. Eventually Truman entered the White House in the last months of World War II, while for a long period Eisenhower seemed indifferent to politics. For that matter, the American public evidenced no great demand for him in that office.

None of these considerations were personal, and that makes them rather important in the White House story, as indication of a trend. No war had produced more distinguished leaders, or more heroes. But in 1948 the Democratic Party rallied around Truman as a candidate for re-election, as its best bet. The Republicans chose Thomas E. Dewey, who had been defeated in 1940 by Roosevelt, but who seemed to wishful-thinking conservatives the best bet to defeat Truman. In fact, at times it seemed that everyone except Truman thought that Dewey could defeat him. But Truman won, and in the subsequent term twice honored Eisenhower by appointments the White House alone could make.

Truman first recalled Eisenhower to Washington to serve in the highest military post, as Chief of Staff from 1945 to 1948. Then Eisenhower retired, to become president of Columbia University, until 1950 when Truman made him Supreme Commander of NATO forces in Europe. In that post Eisenhower would serve until 1952 when, upon being persuaded to stand as a Republican for the

Halloween décor for a luncheon Mrs. Eisenhower gave for the wives of the White House staff

Presidency, he resigned his military commission, and won election as President.

With the Inauguration of Eisenhower in January 1953, the White House again seemed to become—insofar as was possible in this period—an efficient but not particularly glamorous custodian of the 174 nation's responsibilities.

The President, once having chosen his key aides, made it clear that he expected them to handle the responsibilities of their offices, to report to him in short memoranda and not to bother him with details. He ran his office in the manner of his lifetime training, on an organization basis.

In this organization he made one major change, the "promoting" of his Vice President, Richard M. Nixon, to definite rank and responsibility in the Executive establishment, as well as being holder of the constitutional office of presiding officer over the Senate. Thereafter, for eight years, it seemed quite probable that Nixon would succeed Eisenhower, who obviously had this eventuality in mind.

The Vice President thus became a new type of office holder, sitting with the Cabinet, presiding over the Security Council, and therefore as ready as humanly possible to assume the Presidency. This precedent, always of great potential importance, was continued by Kennedy and Lyndon B. Johnson.

Furthermore, the White House exhibited none of the previously feared inclination to bring more of the military into civilian operations. Eisenhower's former senior aides won their promotions until retirement and death thinned their ranks, but always within their services or in positions related to these.

Probably the higest prestige appointment given to a military man by Eisenhower was to Alfred M. Gruenther, his successor as NATO commander, when he approved Gruenther for the position of President of the American National Red Cross in 1956.

However, while the President formally approved the appointment, as provided by law, the selection had been recommended by E. Roland Harriman, Chairman of the Red Cross, who is a leading Republican but who in turn holds his position dating from his initial appointment by Truman.

In the Truman-Eisenhower period, following reconstruction of the White House, there gradually came changes no longer affecting the building or the social and official life within its walls, but which gave the President the space and elbow room sought by all the men who had formerly held that office.

The former State, War, and Navy Building, situated to the west of the White House, was finally cleared of all personnel from those Departments, as these now enormous units found housing in their own huge structures. The Presidential office wing of the White House became just that—workrooms for those closest to the President, and less than a five-minute walk from the newly named Executive Office Building.

The President continued to work in the private office used by his predecessors, and the Cabinet Room was unchanged, but room was found for a larger conference room. In the main section of the White House, the "original" edifice so often altered and restored, the President at last found family privacy above the main floor. There were not only enough bedrooms and guest suites, but also a family dining room. The older small dining room on the main floor became known as the "small state dining room," usable for the lunches and smaller dinners that were part of the President's official entertaining.

There came about also an increase in the White House amenities, some of which reflected ever-growing efforts for better security for the President and some an easier official attitude toward spending money on the White House and the convenience of its current occupant.

A private airplane for the President had become an official arm of the White House soon after Truman became Presi-

The Red Room during the Eisenhower Administration

dent. The Secret Service at last capitulated and decided that airplanes were safe. The first one, still in the pre-jet age, was a massive four-engine plane, named the *Independence,* as a double compliment to a proud word in the nation and to Truman's hometown. With the air section of the Military Transportation Service using hundreds of transports in its world-wide operations, the use of one for the President did not bring any objections, even though operating expenses made the old yacht *Mayflower* seem a cheap toy by comparison.

Sometimes the men who planned such things had to try to anticipate require-

ments to be made on them, and occasionally they got caught in a quandary. During the election of 1948, when the Air Force and almost everyone else thought Dewey would win the election, they prepared a new Presidential private plane, perhaps so that no one would have to use something left over from the outgoing Administration. Word finally leaked out that the plane was named the *Columbia,* and that it was ready and waiting.

With the adaptability of trained tacticians, the Air Force never admitted having such an airplane; in time the old *Independence* was replaced by a new one, which looked to close inquirers exactly

like the *Columbia,* but without that name painted on its side.

Later on the nomenclature was dropped altogether, when the Presidential airplane gained the more dignified but less noticeable name of *Air Force Number One.*

To Eisenhower, these details apparently were of no interest whatsoever. They were so much like his older routine. In his last command post he had long since become accustomed to private airplanes and—something the President has never had—a private train for journeys by land in Europe, as well as fleets of cars, honor guards, and all the trappings of the military who have won wars.

No formal yacht replaced *Mayflower* in the Potomac, but there was something better, from the standpoint of convenience, for river excursions and small dinners on moonlit nights. This was a cruiser about eighty-five feet long, formerly owned by members of the Chrysler family, and taken over by the Navy as an auxiliary patrol boat in World War II. Refitted and painted, it became a luxurious small yacht for the President, and when it was put into new service the name *Margaret* glowed in gilt paint on its stern.

Finally, in the Eisenhower Administration, came the newest of modern wonders added to the White House—helicopters 177

The Rose Room

The Lincoln Room

that landed and took off at a pad only a short walk from the south portico—the final communications link by air between the White House and the world.

Perhaps the helicopters were not an unmixed blessing, because once the landing pad was installed, they became very useful, not only giving the President easy access to his plane at an out-of-town flying field, but also equally convenient for military and other aides to hop over from the Pentagon across the Potomac.

The last in a long line of rest cottages dating from the time when Presidents needed a nearby place in which to escape the worst of the Washington heat was Camp David, a weekend retreat in the hills of western Maryland—named in honor of President Eisenhower's grandson.

Use of such retreats had begun with the borrowing of a cottage on the grounds of Soldiers Home for President Hayes. President Hoover had set up his Virginia fishing cottage in the Shenandoah Mountains on the Rapidan River. Roosevelt had used a resort compound named Shangri-La, and Truman had continued occasional usage of it. Now with Camp David, Eisenhower was equally equipped, and his mountain spot gained its little moment in history when he took Premier Khrushchev to it to discuss plans for a future high-level conference. The "Camp David Agreement" received much publicity, but never reached the point of a meeting.

In the meantime Eisenhower was developing his own project for retirement, made possible by his book *Crusade in Europe,* which made him a relatively wealthy man. This was the estate near Gettysburg, Pennsylvania, where he farms and commutes easily to the historic town and his private offices.

Under a law passed in the last decade, Presidents are paid pensions of $25,000 a year, in addition to relatively small office and secretarial allowances. As a retired General of the Army, Eisenhower qualified for generous but lesser benefits, which he collected during his period as president of Columbia University. During the Presidential period of his service he resigned completely from the Army. But when he served out his terms and retired to private life, President John Fitzgerald Kennedy signed on March 22, 1961, an order restoring the warrior-President to his former military rank on the retirement rolls.

It sometimes seems that the Eisenhower years were either relatively uneventful or that he overshadowed his office and the White House and minimized what otherwise would have been a dramatic period. There seems to be more point to the occasionally heard comment that the Presidency under Eisenhower was an administrative office in which the credit and the blame, as it occurred, glanced off the Executive mansion and always landed in some Department.

This new means of running the White House served on two notable occasions to shield Eisenhower. One was a White House scandal and the other a very touchy diplomatic question.

The scandal involved Sherman Adams, who by his designation as Assistant President was placed by Eisenhower in the chair and the office closest to the seat of power. Adams was so indiscreet as to accept substantial favors from a man doing business with the Government—Bernard Goldfine, of Massachusetts. He resigned, without the incident bruising the President.

In the diplomatic field, Secretary of State John Foster Dulles shocked the United States and the world when, in a speech, he defined "brinkmanship" as a possibly necessary step in foreign policy *vis-à-vis* Communist Russia. The thought of such action as a test of how far America could go without inviting actual warfare quickly disappeared, but the phrase remained to haunt Dulles, not the White House.

As the world and national situation grew more complicated, what once was crisis had become routine, particularly after the truce ending the bitter war in Korea. Yet in these "quiet years," the influence of the White House widened over the world through policy decisions the President alone must make. These decisions which previously might have been made by others concerned local as well as universal dilemmas. For instance, it fell to Eisenhower to order out the first units of the Regular Army, not National Guard enrollees, to enforce one step in desegregation of public schools.

There have been so many developments in the United States's struggle for true integration that now the Little Rock incident has diminished in importance. However, it is a landmark. On September 4, 1957, the White House found it necessary to intervene to uphold both the law and orders from the Federal courts.

As one of the first major tests of State compliance with school desegregation orders, the city of Little Rock, which also is the capital of Arkansas, was ordered to admit nine students to Central High School at the opening of the school year. Governor Orval Faubus ordered State National Guardsmen to the scene, not to enforce the admission of these students, but to prevent their entry.

President Eisenhower personally intervened and invited the Governor to the White House to talk it over, thereby avoiding an immediate show of force. But Faubus declined to accede to that request. In fact, it soon developed, the Governor was more or less helpless in the face of his own prior boasting and was looking for a way out of the dilemma without losing his political strength. It was arranged that a new order be issued by the Federal courts specifically ordering removal of the National Guard. When this red tape was concluded, Faubus took away his little army.

The nine Negro students entered the Little Rock school on September 23 but immediately were ordered out by local authorities on the ground that their admission would lead to mob violence.

On September 24 Eisenhower acted under the seldom-used White House powers to preserve public order when local and state authorities cannot do so or fail to try. He sent in a battalion of soldiers from a training area nearby. It so happened that these men were paratroopers, which added to the sensation, since paratroopers stand out somewhat from other soldiers, wearing bright scarves, heavy boots, and various picturesque insignia. Even though they did not jump their way into Little Rock they looked tough and ready for action.

Of course, there was no action. The city accepted the court orders and admitted the students to integrated classes. The paratroopers were withdrawn. Little Rock returned to calm.

In this narrative of the White House's development as the mirror and focal point of national growth, there is not room for even a sketch of the highlights of the years after World War II. Nevertheless, almost week by week, with restraint under strain and occasional bold action the mansion became the center of Western-world power.

First steps were taken toward helping development of the merging "backward nations," and cooperation was extended to the European powers in their own post-war development. The "space race" with Russia began, coincident with attempts to write treaties limiting testing of atomic bombs. The first satellites were launched by the Soviet Union and by the United States, in that order. In actions of the United States, titular authority or supervision rested with the White House.

It seemed for a time that a new period of "normalcy" had been reached, and that continuance would be assured by the succession of Vice President Nixon to the seat of power.

The Jacqueline Kennedy Garden had been planned but not completed before the assassination of President Kennedy. After his death it was completed and named in Mrs. Kennedy's honor.

The Kennedy Style 18

Critics called John Fitzgerald Kennedy a young man in too much of a hurry, overly ambitious, unfairly equipped with his father's private wealth to wage a fair political campaign, and a man who had neglected the normal responsibilities of his years as a Representative and as a Senator to devote extra time to his quest for the Presidency.

His friends called him a crusader for the human rights that had been submerged too long under efforts to maintain the status quo, noted his personal heroism as a combat veteran, recalled his insight as a writer on history before he started to help make it, and admired his courage for challenging the tradition that no Roman Catholic had been elected President.

His status as a political organizer burst out almost as a surprise when in the 1960 Democratic National Convention he was named as the party's candidate on the first ballot, despite strong preconvention races made by Senator Lyndon B. Johnson and former Presidential candidate Adlai E. Stevenson (or rather, by the supporters of Stevenson).

He was forty-three years old when nominated and it was remarked that if he won the election he would be the youngest man ever elected to the Presidency.

The new contest for the White House aroused unusual interest because it would bring into debate Kennedy and Richard M. Nixon, then rounding out eight years as Eisenhower's Vice President, formerly a popular young Senator from California.

Furthermore, with the country in an era of relative "peace and prosperity" all the odds seemed to favor the candidate of the incumbent party, particularly since he had been hand-picked by Eisenhower.

After winning this nomination, the new candidate made a final run-down of possible Vice Presidential running mates with his younger brother Robert F. Kennedy, who managed his campaign. Then he went around to call on Lyndon B. Johnson to ask him to campaign with him. Johnson demurred briefly, and then accepted the role, although the probability was that the Texan, already in his fifties, was accepting defeat of his own ambition ever to be President. If Kennedy won, Johnson would be out of the accepted age bracket for Presidential nomination eight years later; if Kennedy lost he would simply be another also-ran.

Waiting inconspicuously in the wings was Jacqueline Bouvier Kennedy, in the fifth month of pregnancy, thirty-one years old and mother of a three-year-old daughter named Caroline. Caroline's name would become almost as well known as her father's in the campaign months, because it had been used to christen the airliner identified as "the Kennedy family's private airplane," and which was used largely by the candidate in his campaign. It was doubtful whether this flaunting of great wealth did not hurt the campaign more than the romantic name helped the candidate.

Kennedy won by a hair's breadth in an

election that saw a record number of votes cast—more than 34,000,000 for each major candidate. However, the tradition of "winner take all" in the White House history held firm.

Youth, which revealed a surprisingly tough fiber, took over the White House, and gave to the mansion a new flavor that came to be called "the Kennedy style."

Except for the hard and pragmatic practice of politics, all that had become traditional in a White House occupied for half a century by more mature couples seemed to change. Yet the change was not one generally associated with young occupants. The White House hostess as well as the President brought with them a climate which came to be associated with the more sophisticated atmosphere of serious American youth.

From the earlier years in Congress, the Kennedys had established a Washington background; the Inaugural simply saw them move from a large Georgetown house to the mansion. But their background included much more.

The President, his more intimate biographers have pointed out, was simply fortunate enough to move up the ladder of ambition already established and planned for by his family, whose head—still living at this writing—is Joseph P. Kennedy, financier and former Ambassador under Roosevelt to the Court of St. James's. John Kennedy became the senior son after his older brother was killed while flying in World War II.

But even before he became the oldest Kennedy son among nine children, including five sisters, he was busily studying as

well as living the opulent life provided by his father. In 1935 and 1936, before his father's term as Ambassador, John attended the London School of Economics. He returned home to attend Harvard, where he was graduated as a Bachelor of Science cum laude in 1940. In World War II, on PT boat service, he won Navy and Marine Corps medals and the Purple Heart.

Discharged with serious injury to his back, he worked as a news reporter on assignments at the Potsdam Conference and at the start of the United Nations in San Francisco. By 1947 he had won a seat in the House of Representatives, and in 1952 defeated Henry Cabot Lodge in a race for the Senate.

Twelve years younger than her husband, the new First Lady had a shorter record, but it included studies at Vassar College and the Sorbonne in Paris, culminating in a degree from George Washington University, in Washington, D. C. Although a member of a wealthy family, she worked at times as a newspaper photographer-reporter, on a farm, and as a hospital volunteer. Her languages included French, Spanish, and Italian.

The Kennedy Inaugural was marked by two significant highlights, as regarded the new climate of the White House. First, there was the recitation of an ode by the aging poet Robert Frost, and then an appeal by the new President calling the youth of his generation to a renewal of public service: "My fellow Americans: ask not what your country can do for you —ask what you can do for your country."

On the following March 1 he created by Executive Order the first major step along that line with establishment of the Peace Corps. June found him, accompanied by Mrs. Kennedy, visiting the old guard of European rulers—President de Gaulle in Paris, Prime Minister Harold Macmillan in London, and meeting Premier Khrushchev in Vienna.

In the meantime, the President was no longer referred to by older politicos as "young Kennedy"; he had become a hardened politician asserting his leadership in a manner often compared with Roosevelt's first hundred days in the White House.

The White House saw development of still another new twist, when Kennedy for the first time brought a brother into the Cabinet, with open acknowledgment that his gesture, which some might term nepotism, was made entirely on a practical political plane.

Of Robert Kennedy, he said, "He can have any job he wants, even be Secretary of State." Robert chose a slightly lesser level, that of Attorney General, because of his legal training and interest in pursuing the cause of civil rights. Yet he also was sent abroad on quasi-diplomatic missions.

The two brothers turned out to be a team differing markedly in personalities, but completely compatible in the political structure. The President was urbane, smooth in tailoring and manners; the Attorney General somewhat more sharp in speech, more rumpled and informal— often taking his dog to his office with him.

The formality of the White House as an official residence represented only an extension of the former living customs of John and Jacqueline Kennedy. As Attorney General, Robert and his wife Ethel

A Christmas party for orphans in the State Dining Room, 1961

(then with eight children) lived on a Virginia country estate, teeming with horses and pets of all types.

When the President and the First Lady visited the family "compound" at Hyannisport, Massachusetts, they visited in the house of his father. Robert Kennedy already had erected a large house of his own on these grounds for his growing family.

Both played touch football when out of public observation, and both were skilled yachtsmen, but it was jokingly remarked by friends that when there were family cruises on summer holidays, "Jack and Jackie sat on the afterdeck eating paté and drinking champagne while Bobby and the others had their beer and sandwiches on the foredeck."

In the rash of published material about the Kennedys in the two years prior to this publication so much has been written about politics and statecraft as almost to obscure the unparalleled impact that this President and his family left on the White House. The word "family" is deliberate because no Administration has brought into the White House story so many facets of the American "melting pot." The Kennedy Administration reflected all of them.

Possibly it was because there were so many Kennedys, plus their diverse connections by marriage, all of them individuals in temperament. And the founder of the tribe found time, in the course of many activities, to make the family very wealthy.

Joseph Kennedy celebrated his seventy-seventh birthday anniversary in 1965, partially enfeebled by a stroke. His wife, Rose, celebrated her seventy-fifth birthday anniversary.

They were Boston Irish in their roots and probably their oldest lifelong friend was Cardinal Cushing, of the Boston Archdiocese. The father was a Harvard alumnus and son of a prosperous but not wealthy businessman; the mother was the daughter of a former Mayor of Boston, "Honey" Fitzgerald.

Leaping to financial success, Joseph Kennedy was banker, financier, motion-picture executive, owner of shipping interests, and real estate investor.

By the time of the Roosevelt New Deal, he was able to retire and devote himself to various public offices—retire against a background of big houses in Hyannis Port, Massachusetts, and in Palm Beach, Florida, with a palatial Washington house under lease; yachts, and a private business staff running his affairs from New York offices. He seemingly was "depression proof," and proudly told friends that he had already settled $1,000,000 on each of his children. In 1937 he undertook one of the costliest of foreign assignments, for that period, when Roosevelt named him Ambassador to London.

When John Kennedy became President, his Inaugural was attended by his parents, his two surviving brothers, and three of his four surviving sisters (one of these had died shortly after World War II and the other suffers from an illness that prompted the Kennedys to establish a mental health foundation with what would have been Joseph Jr's. share of the family estate).

The brothers were Robert, already designated for the Cabinet, and Edward, a young lawyer who would become, at thirty years of age, Senator from Massachusetts in 1962, defeating the son of Henry Cabot Lodge, from whom John Kennedy had wrested his own Senate seat in 1952. His sisters were married respectively to: Sargent Shriver, Chicago businessman and soon to be Director of the Peace Corps; Stephen Smith, who is the business manager of the Kennedy interests; and Peter Lawford, the motion-picture star.

The very special member of the family, and the one with the most direct impact on the White House, was Jacqueline. She and her husband would prove to be an extraordinary team in self-discipline, with the President handling the business of the Presidency and Jacqueline managing the White House.

In a brief period of time, the President had to face a blow to United States prestige in the failure of the Bay of Pigs invasion by a small force of Cuban refugees —an action planned, with an assumption of far greater American help, prior to Kennedy's induction into office. Within a year he took full responsibility for an ultimatum demanding removal of Russian missiles from Cuban sites, with the possible alternative of unleashing nuclear war with Russia, and won the gamble.

Concurrently with these actions, and the complicated politics of developing his policy of the New Frontier in extension of desegregation work and enlargement of American opportunities and resources, the White House became a true center of American cultural life.

As hostess of the White House, Jacqueline organized a dinner to which were invited all American winners of Nobel Prizes. Leaders in all fields of the arts from "pop" to classical were made welcome and honored.

Even the Marine Corps Band, senior of the service musical aggregations, and inheritor of the reputation of John Philip Sousa, was inspired with a new idea: its members formed a little group known as the "strolling strings," which wandered through the public rooms at receptions playing light melodies.

Imagination was coupled with the necessary financial means to highlight for guests the historical beauties of the White House and its surroundings. A rose garden, subsequently named by others as a tribute to Jacqueline, was laid out in an area of the lawn immediately behind the President's office. It became a favorite spot later for public ceremonies such as signing of bills, when the weather was favorable. One formal dinner for foreign guests was served on the grounds of Mt. Vernon—the food and service equipment being sent ahead in trucks and buses and the guests proceeding on boats down the Potomac River.

Through all these arrangements, the President moved as host, with proper deference to his wife, but with the dignity becoming a President. He sometimes recalled with amusement his first lesson in protocol taught by an old friend, Mrs. Franklin D. Roosevelt, The story was that she chided him on the first occasion after his Inaugural when it was possible for her to attend a White House dinner in her honor. When service was announced President Kennedy escorted her to the dining-room door, and stood aside. Mrs. Roosevelt halted, and said, "You must learn that the President always goes first."

Thereafter the President always went first, when occasion demanded it, but sometimes a little hesitantly, reminding his friends of his self-conscious reactions when he had to wear a tall silk hat or otherwise conform to the customs of his older confreres. At other times, a sense of humor always close to the surface broke out unexpectedly, as when on his state visit to Paris the most formal of dinners in this old capital was tendered him and his wife.

When the toasts were given, and the important moment came for the President to rise and respond in carefully prepared and rehearsed words from the State Department to the French Foreign Ministry, Kennedy looked up from his notes to make an impromptu introduction recalling the reception that had been given his wife. "I am the man," he said, "who accompanied Jacqueline Kennedy to Paris."

Some of the Kennedy aides have reported in recent years—seemingly interminably and at great profit—on the intense pressure that the President put upon them to fulfill their assignments, and his driving ruthlessness in pursuing the goals of his Administration. But he also introduced a note of informality into the conduct of White House affairs that was greatly at variance with the routines of his older predecessors.

There was the rocking chair, for instance; not some special creation but a simple, old-fashioned rocker, lightly upholstered and comfortable. The rocker became part of the history of the White House, particularly as it had—as in the case of everything concerned with Kennedy—a reason. The rocker was recommended to him because of his wartime injury, and the aggravation of that injury that required subsequent surgery in 1956, when he used his convalescence to write the Pulitzer Prize-winning political profiles, entitled *Profiles in Courage.*

Seated in that rocker Kennedy made much of the history of his Administration, conferred with political leaders invited to office conferences, with diplomats, and with older friends among the press corps with whom he kept up extra-official connections.

Among the friends who adopted his suggestion that a rocking chair supplied a restful posture for thought was his Vice President, Lyndon B. Johnson. The rocking chair, however, was little more than a symbol of the adaptation of the old to the new in changes in the White House— changes back rather than modernization —by which the Kennedys, and particularly Jacqueline, enriched this heritage.

At this point, any current writer is tempted to report that what has been done promises to remain "forever." Perhaps it is better not to predict.

There follows a report of things begun and some completed in 1962.

The newly decorated Green Room

The Treaty Room on the second floor

The new Empire décor of the
Blue Room

Famous paintings on the walls
of the Green Room

The redecorated Red Room

Through the years, the White House has been the victim of various types of neglect and predilections, among which has been a feverish desire to replace the old with something new. In addition there was, for generations, a phobia—beginning right after the Civil War—of spending Government money on objects which were not made in America. This affected not only the White House, but all Government buildings, and so prevented that blending of the old and new that has marked the development of the finest American taste.

A revolt against this tendency began with the reconstruction of the building in the Truman Administration, but Jacqueline Kennedy gave an aggressive leadership to the work of retrieving what could be saved from the past, and the fitting of it into a unified pattern. The hope of pre-

serving and improving upon this work lies with a White House Fine Arts Commission that is now a permanent institution. The following is a summation of the accomplishments in this latest restoration.

The structure whose picture is familiar to almost everyone sits in a tree-shaded area of eighteen acres, fronting north toward Pennsylvania Avenue and south toward the artificial hill erected long ago as the site for the Washington Monument. A few of the trees on the grounds are survivors of the elms originally planted by Thomas Jefferson.

The main building, which now has six floors including the basement, is 170 feet long and 85 feet wide from north to south, exactly as Hoban proportioned it in his plans. To the east runs a terrace 135 by 35 feet, leading to the east wing, a three-story building 139 by 82 feet, facing the

With a trend toward less formality, President Kennedy replaced other furniture with these two large sofas and a coffee table near the big fireplace in his office

Treasury Building. This has offices upstairs and the formal entrance for official receptions, following the lines laid out by McKim, Mead, and White in 1902.

To the west is a companion terrace 174 by 35 feet that leads to the office wing, three stories high, and 148 by 98 feet, built in 1902 and enlarged several times in later years. This office wing, which faces the Executive Office Building, has already been described; it is supplemented by other offices in the west terrace, and also includes the swimming pool built as a present from children to Franklin D. Roosevelt.

As now viewed from Pennsylvania Avenue, the building is a continuous structure running from curb to curb of the bordering east and west streets, which are named East Executive Avenue and West Executive Avenue. The south

grounds, with a greater area than that which faces Pennsylvania Avenue, are bordered by a curving driveway.

Within these walls Mrs. Kennedy undertook to work with and sponsor the group known as the White House Historical Association in recapturing all that was possible from the best of the past. Her principal adviser was John Walker, who was until 1956 Curator of the National Gallery of Art, and a noted authority on Americana. Finally, she and Walker wrote a guidebook entitled *The White House,* which is sold to the public. Receipts from it provide funds for special details aside from official purchases.

Some of these "details" involve extraordinary work and expense. As an example, two years were required to weave and make new draperies for the East Room, installed in the first week of Sep-

The Family Dining Room

tember 1965. These draperies, of classical detailed design on gold-colored damask, are sixteen feet long and cost $25,000.

The East Room, which remains in general appearance much as it has for more than half a century, is a great reception room, with comparatively little furniture. The Kennedy program was more concerned with the smaller rooms, whose furniture and furnishings make their character. There are about a dozen of these, divided half between the ground floor, on the level with the East Room, and the second floor.

Through these have been scattered the principal items of valuable Americana and fine imports from earlier periods, largely contributed by others in the restoration program.

The most formal and probably most gracefully proportioned room designed by Hoban is the historic Blue Room, which every President has used as his formal reception room. It is oval in shape, with an uncovered and polished parquet floor. Blue and gold silk fabric covers the walls on which are hung portraits of Monroe and Jackson, but of greatest interest to visitors are the furnishings: original chairs, a pier table, a French clock and candlesticks of gilt bronze preserved since 1817 when the Monroes ordered French furniture of this excellent period for the rebuilt White House.

The adjoining Green Room, designated for use for informal receptions, recaptures the American Federal style. Green damask on the walls is set off by a white marble fireplace and white enameled wainscoting and door trim. Among the furniture is a sofa once owned by Daniel Webster and a pair each of rare American settees and chairs. The central point of attention in this room is a portrait of Benjamin Franklin, painted in 1767 and donated to the White House in 1962, which is valued at an estimated $200,000. This is probably the most valuable work of art in the building except possibly the Gilbert Stuart portrait of George Washington in the East Room, which was rescued by Dolley Madison.

The third formal parlor, the Red Room, is furnished in the Empire period of European decoration—more or less contemporary with the Madison-Monroe era—but more noted as a portrait gallery than for its unusual furnishings. Among the unique items are an old Aubusson carpet, a sofa once owned by Dolley Madison and another from the home of Nellie Custis Lewis, a granddaughter of Martha Washington.

The portraits in the Red Room span a long period: from Thomas Jefferson, among the Presidents, through Taylor, Theodore Roosevelt, Wilson, Hoover, F. D. Roosevelt, and Truman. Also present are Commodore Barry and Chief Justice John Marshall.

Probably the most striking feature of this heavily laden room is the covering of the walls that carry out its name—cerise silk with gold scroll borders.

In the State Dining Room, the Kennedy redecoration principally restored the walls to their original lighter tones—clear oak paneling set off by the Corinthian pilasters painted white, instead of the previous darker tints. This room is mainly space—large enough to seat 120 persons, as it was designed to do in 1902, at a main table and at surrounding smaller ones, with chairs (not antique) in the styles known as Queen Anne and William and Mary.

The State Dining Room with tables set for 120 guests

The main dining-room table has for a centerpiece another of the Monroe acquisitions, a French bronze-doré plateau. The dinner service, which sooner or later will have to be replaced, was purchased in the Truman Administration.

Little could be done to the Small State Dining Room, used for entertaining at breakfasts and luncheons, but on its walls was hung a portrait of President Tyler, not because of Tyler's distinction as President but because he happened to be painted by the famous George Healy.

The Diplomatic Reception Room was turned into a record for history during the Eisenhower Administration, through gifts

made by the National Society of Interior Designers. Here, in this large entrance for people invited to state receptions, is scenic wallpaper based on engravings made in 1820 and a modern Aubusson rug into whose pattern are woven the seals of the fifty States.

Also on the ground floor is the library, a relatively small room, designed to illustrate the painted decoration of an early American room. Its walls are yellow and the moldings are cream-colored. The furniture is a mixture of styles, and on the wall is an old French painting which depicts the signing of the Declaration of Independence.

The White House Diplomatic Reception Room as changed by the Kennedys

With the addition of further private quarters for the Presidential families in the Coolidge Administration, when the new roof was needed, a number of rooms not now connected with the President's office but historical and interesting in their older associations, ·have been redesigned to illustrate their place in the mansion's history.

Best known of these is the Lincoln Bedroom—as it is now called—and in which Lincoln is popularly supposed to have slept in a huge bed, ornately carved, with corresponding Victorian furniture. Actually Lincoln did not sleep in the bed. This was his Cabinet Room, and the furni-

ture was in a guest room. But here he did sign the Emancipation Proclamation in 1863. On the wall is a Jackson portrait that he admired, and there is a copy of the Gettysburg Address, copied out in his own handwriting, that came to the White House as a gift under the will, in 1957, of Oscar B. Cintas, former Ambassador from Cuba to the United States.

Next door to the Lincoln Bedroom is the Treaty Room, which was used by Jackson, and some of his successors after Lincoln, as the Cabinet Room. The treaty of peace with Spain was signed in this room in 1899. Now used as a writing room or occasional meeting room by the

President, it does have several old pieces of Victorian furniture and a number of paintings, including one of Lincoln and Grant in conference, another of McKinley signing the treaty with Spain, and portraits of Andrew Johnson, Grant, and Taylor.

The President's dining room, on the second floor, which seems relatively small and intimate only by comparison with the larger state rooms, is charmingly decorated with scenic blue wallpaper, blue hangings at the windows, Federal period furniture and an Empire chandelier.

Two other rooms, bedrooms on the second floor, are gathering their own history. One is the Rose Guest Room, specially reserved for distinguished women guests. In it have slept the Queen Mother Elizabeth of Great Britain, Queen Elizabeth II, and Queens Wilhelmina and Juliana of the Netherlands and Frederika of Greece.

The Empire Guest Room has walls and upholstery of red and white printed cotton showing scenes from the life of Benjamin Franklin, and a "sleigh bed" that is believed to have been owned by John Quincy Adams.

All in all, this is now an impressive and a graceful house, a repository of mementoes from the past, but one with the privacy and dignity suitable to the country's First Citizen. Yet the old seems to furnish a harsh contrast to the new when occasionally the vibrations from the helicopters rattle panes in the windows.

This is a summary of the White House as redone in its most recent overhaul, and a story shown and told for the first time on television, when Jacqueline Kennedy appeared as "hostess" to show the work to millions of viewers.

This seemed to be a climax of the modern chapter of the White House story, the report of the retailoring of the old mansion in decent historical perspective to the needs of modern living and a modern Administration. All seemed settled for a reasonable period of time, for the gradual mellowing of a new and youthful leadership into the stable line of American history.

The crises seemed less urgent against such a background, and social and economic problems more endurable and conquerable. Democracy could be both sharp and fast in repelling threats, and also well rooted in these evidences of its past.

Then the whole picture of the New Frontier as personified by the Kennedys exploded violently. On November 22, 1963, while riding in a motorcade through Dallas, Texas, with Jacqueline at his side, the President was killed by a bullet fired at long range from an assassin's rifle.

A ballet in the East Room

In the fleeting hours of the night following the assassination, the stature of the White House both as symbol and heart of our Government grew into proportions never reached before that time. And the events demonstrated how modern communications have broadened its activities from the banks of the Potomac to universal enclosure of American interests.

No one knew whether Kennedy had been assassinated at the whim of a mad individual or as part of a plot against the whole Government. No one knew, for that matter, how the Vice President would react to the new stresses thrown upon him. His forte had been that of legislation—compromise, deals, and leadership in the Senate. He had shown, lacking the opportunity, little of the diplomatic finesse that had come to mark the "Kennedy style." Yet many of the questions were to be answered within a few hours.

Aboard *Air Force Number One,* where he took the oath of office, attendants loaded a coffin. Then the new President's wife and the late President's widow, took their seats in silence, an air guard covering the skies above the United States to protect this plane swung into patrols, and the new President sat down in the plane's "office" to begin marathon telephoning through the White House switchboard.

There were honors to be paid to the dead, with extreme consideration for his family, and the preparations for the memorial service. Yet within the working enclave of the White House there was the serious business of the work required to keep the continuity of functioning government, plus preparations to forestall any potential efforts by enemies to take advantage of this tragedy.

Fortunately, by the planning of his chief, the new President had been abroad and had met many of the heads of state with whom he must now deal as an equal. But his travels had been those of a deputy or stand-in for the White House leadership. Now, many of these dignitaries came to see him in his new role and, while observing the amenities of honoring the dead President, to extend careful feelers for new attitudes and policy changes.

They met a Texan who from the start demonstrated how big an American a Texan can be.

When Johnson became Vice President, there was a spate of cartoons and humorous comment about the LBJ brand, and the manner in which he had impressed it upon his family, his home, and his surroundings. He made his own initials suit his wife, whom he had long ago given the nickname Lady Bird, and their daughters Luci and Lynda had been christened with names containing the letter B as a middle initial. "It makes it easy," Johnson had said, "for us all to use the same luggage."

People had noticed that Johnson had been a dynamic politician for the majority of his adult years spent on Capitol Hill: first as an employee, then as a member of the House of Representatives and in more recent years as a Senator. But outside of Texas few had realized how much he epitomized the go-getter spirit of his region.

Working with Mrs. Johnson's inheritance of $60,000, together the Johnsons had built up the small empire of a millionaire, including radio and television properties and a ranch around the house where the President was born. They had modernized and enlarged the ranch so much over the years that the new President was able to have a private airplane and crew that operated from a landing strip on the ranch. It suddenly dawned on people who had not been intimate with Johnson that he was nearly as well off as had been Kennedy.

While it was no longer necessary for a man to be wealthy to be President, there was some reassurance in the fact that this new President would not be overawed by the accouterments of his new environment. And there were, of course, the other questions as to how Johnson could have made "all that money" by just sitting in Congress, until detailed explanations quieted the curious.

The rules of the political game surrounding the White House gave Johnson a few weeks less than one year to demonstrate whether he was a man capable of following in the footsteps of Teddy Roosevelt and Truman, or whether he would join the secondary ranks of Van Buren, Andrew Johnson, and Chester A. Arthur among the "caretaker" Presidents who had unexpectedly followed their deceased predecessors into the White House.

The answers provided by Johnson's actions in the little more than two years preceding the writing of this story would seem overwhelming in his favor. And therein is to be found a monumental compliment to the evolution that has occurred in the whole White House procedure developed in less than a generation. It may be part of the coming of age of the United States.

The political parties seem to have begun to realize that the Vice President is just that, a man carefully chosen to succeed a President—that whatever the stamp of the party's policies the White House is too important to trust to the health and safety of a single individual. However great Johnson's future as President may be, he owes a certain debt to Kennedy for selecting him as a running mate, just as Eisenhower had been equally careful in selecting and training for possible succession of Richard Nixon. On the same basis, although it took a little while for recognition, Johnson selected Hubert Humphrey as his running mate, and then went on to place Humphrey not in the seat of power but in the very center of the intricate web of activities that make up the always expanding White House routine.

The Kennedy and Johnson Administrations, so different in their individual personalities, are yet the latest and most graphic examples of the ponderous and yet delicate balance upon which the reputation and the prestige of the White House rests.

Each new President and each successive First Lady is a prisoner of what has become a long tradition. And at the same time, each succeeding First Family must bring an individuality to the mansion or suddenly find that it is out of step with the times. When men have not been elected in their own right, it is at first doubly difficult. Perhaps it is safe, at this time, to say that in our generation—especially under the bright lights of television —the Johnsons have succeeded, or so it seems to this reporter.

Even with the "closeness" under modern White House procedure, the Vice President actually lives at arm's length

President Johnson stops to shake hands with tourists during one of his walks around the White House grounds

He had become master of a house about whose intimate nuances he really was only a little better informed than many of the other leaders of his Party. But from that moment he was expected to carry forward successfully and dynamically every detail of the New Frontier, realizing that every one of these details would be critically examined in the light of whether he had done it as well as Kennedy would have performed.

On the whole, he did, and that marked his first Administration. Then, after the election of 1964, he was expected to become an entirely different kind of President. His critics would have been delighted to term him a carbon copy of his predecessor, a do-nothing or second-rater elected perhaps because of the extraordinary failures of the opposition candidate.

Thus Johnson had to branch out on his own, as he did with his blueprint for the Great Society; to be strong as he had to be in handling the Vietnam crisis; to become a world leader in economic and political affairs. His success or failure would either enhance the dignity of the institution or bring chaos and uncertainty to the entire country.

For the present, there are three White Houses, separate in space but through modern communications all functioning simultaneously.

First, there is, of course, the traditional White House on the banks of the Potomac, sitting at the heart of a global network of problems, communications, and intelligence. The second is the ranch house on the banks of the Pedernales River, in Texas, linked by air, highway, and tele-

from the President, principally because of the necessary security procedures. He meets formally and occasionally in the heavily guarded Cabinet sessions or those of the Security Council and similar groups. But he rarely has the opportunity to engage in long informal talks with the President. They never travel on the same airplane or train, or in the same automobile. They almost never attend the same public or private meetings. They are never supposed to be in a place where one bomb or one accident can simultaneously eliminate both. It was a very rare thing—and due only to the Texas political situation—that Johnson was with Kennedy in Dallas at all.

Hence, the almost frantic summoning of men to conferences that Johnson began by telephone on his politically and emotionally lonely first flight as President.

phone to the "Texas White House" in the Federal Office Building in Austin. The third White House is in the air, in a jet airplane so equipped as to have been unbelievable even in F. D. Roosevelt's era.

From the standpoint of the White House business, there no longer is much difference, except for convenience of personal contact, in which chair the President happens to be sitting at a given moment. In Washington more people can answer his summons to a visit or a conference in a shorter time, but the difference is only in hours and he can divide his time among so many people a day.

The LBJ Ranch, through the use of jet airplanes, has been found to be almost too close for comfort for scores of Executive Department officials summoned there for conferences from their own planned weekends or other holiday periods.

Wherever the President sits, he can press a button, or pick up the telephone (even in his personal car speeding across the countryside) and talk to anyone anywhere. And close beside him—perhaps allowing for lapses of a few minutes—are others, such as the custodian of the secret codes, who practically sleep outside his door.

With communications scramblers he talks and sends to the central White House offices messages that cannot be "tapped" from the air. Reports from the world's trouble spots can reach him with speed that almost daily becomes more unbelievable.

When the accelerated bombing against Viet Cong positions was first ordered in Vietnam—here again a decision that had to be and could be taken only by the

A press conference in the East Room

President—Johnson appeared unusually preoccupied while entertaining a small group of officials at a dinner conference. One of them commented on LBJ's mood and asked why he was not joining in the more social aspects of the party after dinner. "I'm sorry," Johnson remarked, "but I've got my bombers out tonight, and I'm not going to take a drink until they're reported back."

This was spoken by a man in Washington, prepared to be in instant communication with the command that had dispatched a force of B-52 bombers from bases in Okinawa to strike halfway across southern Asia at a pinpoint target south of China.

The more amazing thing was that this could be accepted as routine. Beyond that, the routine would have been as easily maintained had the President's "office" 203

Tourists watch President Johnson take off in a helicopter

been adjacent to his lounge in *Air Force Number One,* or in Austin with open telephone lines to the LBJ Ranch.

But even in the midst of his elaborate office arrangements in Washington, the older procedures and accommodations have seemed to be too confining for this Texan. His innovations even in the first year of his own term seemed radical compared with those introduced by Kennedy.

It seems only a little more than the day before yesterday when the first press conferences were televised to a live audience directly from Washington. These were rather ponderous in the use of obviously prepared statements and with a few answers to equally obviously prepared questions. They were not press conferences at all, in the meaning of the word derived from the beginnings in F.D.R.'s time, when relatively small groups of newspapermen asked questions at will, got an-

swers on or off the record, and in the aggregate collected impressions as important as the spoken replies.

The televised press conference, staged in the old State Department Auditorium —now part of the White House offices— were closely similar in type, although more frequent, than the grand televised receptions periodically held by de Gaulle.

Under the Kennedy management, the televised press conference became in time less formal, and he made a reputation for sagacity in the manner in which he fielded large numbers of spontaneous questions.

Lyndon Johnson picked up the challenge and the technique, with a success that won compliments, but then added to it a revival of the older type of press conference, when it suited his own aims and purposes. (Always remember that no newspaperman has lived long under the illusion that press conferences are for the benefit of reporting mediums; to every President they have been a means of communicating policy for the benefit of the Administration.)

While Johnson perpetuated the televised press conference, in response to demands from the massive press corps, he suddenly began to send word to the regularly assigned men in the White House press room, with an invitation to join him when he thought the timing propitious. Thus again conversations could be held without the benefit or limitation of vast numbers of television viewers or radio listeners looking over the reporters' shoulders.

Then with the coming of mild weather in the spring of 1965, Johnson took the press corps outdoors for constitutionals on the White House grounds that might last up to two hours. A restless and vigorous man, sometimes taking his dogs on leash, he would make the rounds of the grounds, talking, answering questions, and having a wonderful visit with men and women correspondents who perspiringly raced to keep up with him, while endeavoring to make notes of the unexpected remarks by the President.

There were moments of rest when the President stopped to shake hands through the fence with tourists who seemed to know by some instinct that he might be passing by. The Secret Service men assigned to protect the President try to keep these hand-shaking pauses to a minimum because they cannot possibly protect him if even a single crank tried to attack him.

Then came another development, as Johnson—working with the skill of an impresario in the game of political staging —came as close as possible to bringing television and other communications into all of his promotion plans, publicizing everything from the signing of bills to the reporting of events as they occurred.

In fact, the television companies cried for help at one point, pointing to the dislocation of so many programs on regular schedules and the costs they were incurring in handling these broadcasts at any hour of day or evening. They refrained from direct complaint, but intimated quite clearly that many hours were provided for news announcements and that it would be helpful if the President would refrain as much as possible from pre-empting the costliest hours for his public announcements.

There was some change, but not much

President Johnson and the Joint Chiefs of Staff in the Presidential office

in 1965. The President himself was deeply involved in broadcasting, until he temporarily shelved his active business interests while serving in the White House. No one really expected that he would wait for secondary time when he wanted to broadcast.

In one of his more dramatic stagings, he asked for and got on the air shortly before 7 P.M. on a fall evening in 1965 to announce settlement of the then impending steel strike, and take before the cameras the negotiators he was thanking—the men he had dramatically "invited" earlier to go into a suite in the Executive Office Building and remain there until they reached agreement.

There were no beds in the suite, where they remained for more than two days, but they ate fairly well, with meals served from the White House kitchens. The President commented to the television au- *205*

The White House bowling alley provides relaxation for White House employees

The lobby in the West Wing, newly refurbished in 1965

dience, "We gave them lunches so they wouldn't get too hungry, and light dinners so they wouldn't get too sleepy at night."

This broadcast incidentally was made from the East Room of the White House, as part of the Johnson peripatetic changes of background for his broadcasts. In the balmier weather of the mild seasons, Johnson has publicly signed bills in the Rose

Garden under bright skies, in his office, and in the East Room. He has gone to Capitol Hill to sign them there, and he has signed them under the Texas sky at the LBJ Ranch.

One newspaper feature writer, whose sense of humor had been tested by more than forty years of Presidential idosyncra-cies, wrote a piece under the title, "Have Pens, Will Sign Bills."

These signings have been for many years a prerogative of Presidential pub-licity—used on high occasions for public approval of measures, in which the Chief Executive would use several pens to write parts of his signature.

Johnson lifted the total of pens to new heights, as he frequently dipped, made a mark with, and presented more than one hundred wooden pens to sponsors or in-terested participants in single pieces of legislation.

He always made the pens come out right, but his signature occasionally seemed to be more ornate than at other times. If his name could not be stretched through the pens, even with the making of a tiny stroke with each one, he would add flourishes at the end or fill in with serifs on the letters.

But these ceremonial demonstrations never seemed to detract from the hard-driving determination of this latest Presi-dent to hammer through a record that would excel any of his predecessors, and to make an additional mark as keeper of the peace and freedom in the world.

Within a few months after the settling of the furor surrounding Johnson's elec-tion to the Presidency in his own right, there came another pronounced change in the character of the White House occupancy. Possibly it heralded the opening of another era. The new First Lady, Lady Bird Johnson, began to emerge as a personality, not rivaling her predecessors, but establishing her own distinctive role.

She continued in a limited manner the encouragement of leaders in the arts, such as sponsorship in the summer of 1965 of an all-American art show on the White House grounds. At the same time, there came touches reminiscent of Mrs. Franklin D. Roosevelt in going directly to the public in a personal campaign to promote conservation of national resources for parks and recreational facilities.

Illustrating the change in status of Presidential wives, no critical voice was raised—at least with sufficient force to be noticeable—about this campaign. This was due probably both to the change in atmosphere as well as to careful planning of strategy, assisted by the President and bearing evidence of a widespread planning of promotion.

The most eye-catching part of the publicity consisted of several pictures of Mrs. Johnson—a shapely and very youthful matron—in the national parks, particularly when she was attired in one costume of pull-over sweater, slacks, and hiking boots. Due conservatism was lent to this picture by the presence of Lady Bird's walking companions, Mr. and Mrs. Laurence Rockefeller.

In the background of this campaign, which she waged while legislation to advance the objective was pending in the Congress, were other powerful collaborators. Among them were Supreme Court Justice William O. Douglas, by hobby a famous naturalist and conservationist, and Secretary of the Interior Stuart Udall.

This activity by the First Lady may have been surprising to the public, but to her friends it seemed only natural. Her unexpected elevation to White House position, alongside her husband, had suddenly cut out from under her a career in business built up continuously since 1942, and had relegated her to the ranks of the unemployed.

Some readers will recall the furor during Eisenhower's first campaign when questions were raised about Richard M. Nixon's financial resources and how he had acquired them. His explanations, made dramatically in a television appearance, were satisfactory and above reproach, but thereafter each Presidential candidate, and some Vice Presidential ones, have made full disclosures of their financial affairs.

Kennedy set a precedent by putting into trusteeship his private fortune, where it remained until his death. On his succession, Johnson did the same thing, but in his case, parts of the fortune were owned by Mrs. Johnson and their daughters, Lynda and Luci, and Mrs. Johnson was the active head of all business affairs. Suddenly she was no longer chief of the broadcasting interests, and the ranching, timber, and other properties—all of which went into management outside the control of the President or members of his immediate family.

It was not enough for this woman in her early fifties to settle back into a routine of membership on charity committees and the planning of social engagements.

Besides, her predecessor, Jacqueline Kennedy, had about exhausted the possibilities of "doing" the White House.

With the Johnsons' occupancy of the mansion, there was restored after a lapse of about fifty years the atmosphere of a family with young daughters—the first since Woodrow Wilson's election. Of these in 1965 the elder, Lynda, went off to a university in another city, but Luci, upon graduation from high school, enrolled for a four-year course in nursing at Georgetown University Medical School, a local Washington institution. That meant a degree of year-round junior activity under the White House roof.

In order to give some idea of teen-age festivities in the otherwise formal old house, the President and Mrs. Johnson permitted in the fall of 1965 a television program showing a party given by Luci. (The commentary contained an explanation that Luci is highly competent in the frug and the Watusi, but that her parents decided against her being pictured doing them.) The party illustrated in another way the unexpected parallels in usage of the mansion in informal moments. It was held in a large room on the upper floor, arranged so that "outdoor" grilling could be done, as well as dancing. The room, it was explained, had been improvised first by President Eisenhower as a convenient place to indulge his hobby of grilling steaks over charcoal.

To those who have watched the Johnson mode of life developing in the White House, however, there have come occasional expressions of sympathy for the daughters, because of new legal restrictions put into effect after the assassination of Kennedy, and the usual crank threats habitually sent to the President.

An absolute rule was laid down—not subject to veto by the President—that he and members of his family should never be out of sight of trained guards from the Secret Service. For that matter, the same rules were made for the former Presidents and their immediate families—to the expressed irritation in particular of Harry Truman.

But for Lynda and Luci it meant that wherever they went, and whatever they did, privately or as members of their parents' official parties, they were never unguarded.

Luci commented, "Do you know that if Lynda or I get married while our father still is President we never will have had a moment alone with our fiancés?"

In actual fact, it might be arranged at home, because the guard rule, requiring personal presence, is relaxed within the rooms of the family quarters on the second floor.

Despite these limitations, there were other changes exemplified by the daughters that showed the degree to which tolerance has grown and snobbery has declined in the average range of American thinking and its attitude mirrored in the White House.

It was unusual, by the standards even of the recent 1940s, that Luci caused little comment by enrolling in a school for nurses instead of a more orthodox college specializing in the liberal arts, or perhaps one of the sciences.

More of a breath-taker, by any but the most recent views of prejudice, was Luci's quiet decision to adopt the Roman Catholic faith as her religion. Of course, Kennedy had been a Roman Catholic, the first of his religion to occupy the White House, but that had been fought out in the atmosphere of politics. Luci's decision, entirely her own, was approved as a personal one by her father, a member of the Church of Christ, and her mother, an Episcopalian. It was simply an example of the growth of mind and intelligence in the United States that Luci's decision caused no more than a ripple of interest.

In its role as mirror of American development, the White House reflected another precedent, which history indicates will no longer be subject to question.

This was remarked by the President later in 1965 when the unexpected death of Adlai E. Stevenson vacated the office of Chief of the United States Mission to the United Nations, and Johnson asked Arthur Goldberg to resign from the Supreme Court to accept appointment to this post. Justice Goldberg had served in line with a tradition of many decades that one Justice on that court should be a Jew, but the UN post is very special, as it uniquely combines major ambassadorial status with Cabinet membership.

In a television program introducing Mr. Goldberg as UN appointee, President Johnson made a point of his own relative minority status when he said, "When a Southerner can be elected President of the United States, a Jew can be appointed to represent our country at the United Nations, and Negroes can aspire to the highest appointive offices in the nation, I think we have a record of which we can be proud."

Since all chronological accounts such as this one necessarily must end before the date of their publication, this one closes on a high note of promise for the future, insofar as the White House story is concerned.

The narrative will now turn to summarization and some attempt at perspective in the roles of the White House as symbol, office, and tool of the historic line of Presidents and their families.

Three paragraphs written in less than three hundred words in the Constitution outline, as the responsibilities of the President, all the powers of the vast establishment now indicated in the description of "the White House."

Section 2. The President shall be Commander in Chief of the Army and Navy of the United States, and of the Militia of the several States, when called into the actual Service of the United States; he may inquire the Opinion, in writing, of the principal Officer of each of the Executive Departments, upon any subject relating to the duties of their respective Offices, and he shall have power to grant Reprieves and Pardons for Offenses against the United States, except in Cases of Impeachment.

He shall have power, by and with the Advice and Consent of the Senate, to make Treaties, provided two-thirds of the Senators present concur; and he shall nominate, and by and with the Advice and Consent of the Senate, shall appoint Ambassadors, other public Ministers and Consuls, Judges of the Supreme Court, and all other Officers of the United States, whose Appointments are not herein provided for, and which shall be established by Law; but the Congress may by Law vest the Appointment of such inferior Officers, as they think proper, in the President alone, in the Courts of Law, or in the Heads of Departments.

The President shall have Power to fill up all Vacancies that may happen during the Recess of the Senate, by granting Commissions which shall expire at the end of their next Session.

That is the power of the White House as it always has been and is now under the Constitution. All that has occurred since to enhance and enlarge the White House as the third arm of the Federal Government has been built upon expediency, the varying personalities of the Presidents, and the changing moods of Congress reflected in the granting of emergency powers.

The story has been recounted, and accepted as fact, that George Washington first broached the limits of the Constitution after a hectic evening with a group of Senators debating the questions of current foreign affairs.

Washington reportedly listened to their arguments with the patience of his disciplined background. However, when his guests had departed he was said to have exclaimed that he would be damned if he would ever again "advise" with the Senate; that it could have its say when and if his conduct of foreign affairs reached the point of a treaty.

The anecdote was revived and told in many versions after Woodrow Wilson attempted to reach advance agreements on the League of Nations proposals with his Senate adversaries.

As one precedent has been piled upon another, the White House today is a seat of power in foreign affairs that—aside from a few dictatorships that may be considered transitory, including Charles de Gaulle's French regime—has no parallel.

Presidents "purchased" Louisiana, Florida, and Alaska and carried their deals to a point of finality before laying these before the Senate or the Congress for approval. The Texas war for independence was won with American help before it reached the stage of annexation and formal war with Mexico.

The Spanish-American War was clearly based on a declaration of war by the Congress as a result of destruction of the battleship *Maine* in Havana. But both World Wars I and II were declared to be formal wars only after a long series of events in each case conducted solely within the discretion of White House authority.

Since those now relatively long-ago events, a succession of approved treaties has given the successive Presidents virtually life-and-death power to engage in foreign conflicts, subject only to the later approval by the Congress of appropriations needed to carry out these decisions.

The White House in the 1960s is somewhat comparable to the British crown a century ago when, as Winston Churchill wrote, Britain's efforts to assure relative peace in the world forced it to stumble unwittingly into possession of an Empire.

Now there is a new "empire," not put together by planned conquest, or by any single President or political party in the United States, but existing rather as the result of almost frantic efforts to shore up the walls protecting peace.

If there was a formal beginning to this accretion of power and authority, it was the Monroe Doctrine, for which principal responsibility has been given to John Quincy Adams when he was Monroe's Secretary of State. This pronouncement—not even a treaty subject to Senate approval—warned other countries to keep hands off Latin America.

Most Americans have forgotten the next significant move, taken by Theodore Roosevelt, when saber-rattling among Europe's major powers threatened war, and he had the bulk of the American fleet that had defeated Spain painted white and sent around the world as an example of American power for maintaining the peace. In the same period, Teddy started construction of the Panama Canal by devious negotiations preceding Congressional approval. He later boasted, "I took the Canal Zone and let Congress debate, and while the debate goes on the canal does also."

The power of the White House seemed irreparably shorn, with defeat of the League of Nations and the proposal for the United States to adhere to the World Court, but this turned out to be a temporary pause.

As a result of World War II, there came first the United Nations with its hopeful promises, yet committing the United States prior to any Congressional approval to the co-defense of all its members. And when the UN became a shaky organization in the face of Soviet-American conflict, there grew the other commitments such as NATO, binding the United States to defense of its European allies under the sole judgment of the President, and SEATO, covering friendly nations in southeastern Asia and numerous subsidiary agreements. Finally came another agreement covering Latin America—somewhat disputed in its broad terms—giving the United States presumed power to defend the Western Hemisphere (exclusive of Canada, a British Commonwealth country) against armed incursions by Communist forces.

By this time, at this writing, it seemed

unlikely that there would ever be another "war" involving the United States in the old formal sense of the word; in effect, it seemed more likely that major war, if it occurred, would be started and perhaps finished before Congress could get around to debating it.

Truman had directed the defense of South Korea as a commitment of the United States to the United Nations, and had faced the crisis of the first Soviet land blockade of Berlin; Eisenhower settled the Korean truce and directed the agreements that later would lead to the undeclared war building up over a period of years in Vietnam; Kennedy spent many anxious hours purely on his own responsibility after warning Russia to remove newly installed rockets in Cuba or face atomic bomb annihilation, a problem that Johnson inherited along with addition of a revolution in Santo Domingo.

So the merry-go-round whirled. A reporter observed, "About all that Congress had left in its control was the money."

The marvel of it all was how smoothly the system continued to work.

In domestic affairs the growth and changes in the Federal establishment have, in a single generation prior to this writing, changed the Presidency from a personal office in responsibilities to an organization of activities over which he holds direct responsibility and for which he is directly accountable.

It is as though the President sits in what long ago was termed "splendid isolation" on top of a pyramid, which constantly grows with enlargement at the base and raises him higher and higher into the area of lonely responsibilities.

If these responsibilities were only few in number and dramatic, like his individual control over potential unleashing of atomic bombs, or decisions to throw military power into isolated conflicts in foreign areas, or to declare "emergencies" in time of natural disasters, his powers would be unique.

However, the White House is the center of a thousand anthills of activities, about which the President must keep at least well enough informed to defend politically when necessary, to staff responsibly, and to stimulate to high activity.

Herbert Hoover, in his Administration, was the first President to realize that the White House had become in its operations the most obsolete activity in government. His reorganization at that time, and his two great surveys subsequently, began the reforms of the President's office, laying groundwork for the expansion caused principally by World War II.

In the house itself, as immediate changes, Mr. Hoover did what only a man of considerable wealth could afford. Under the Budget he was allocated one secretary and a small clerical staff. The secretary was paid $7,500 a year, and all of the others less. Hoover raised the official secretary's salary to $10,000, added two other secretaries at the same salary, and gave more realistic raises in salary to a number of other employees. All of the added cost was paid for a while out of his private funds.

This was the beginning of the White House practice of having three secretaries   *213* to handle respectively appointments, press information, and liaison with Congress.

Roosevelt got the money appropriated to carry on the same enlargement, but as the Federal establishment grew with the emergency and relief programs, he found more and more spots in established Departments and agencies for the men who worked as closely or more closely with him than the Department Secretaries, whose establishments also were growing apace. Thus Harry Hopkins, despite numerous titles, always was in fact Roosevelt's intimate deputy.

Up to the period of hectic months marking the emergency period prior to World War II, the President could and did keep in normal touch with operations of the Executive Establishment through meetings with members of his Cabinet, but soon the Cabinet members themselves —particularly State and the military— found themselves so swamped with detail that they required greater time for concentration on their jobs.

The White House began to develop more "personal assistants" to the President, to keep track of specific programs, to gather information for programs that crossed over Department limits, and sometimes to recommend Presidential action in areas very close to infringement on Cabinet responsibilities.

In 1965 the President received authority from Congress to add to the White House establishments a Department of Urban Affairs, but this made no real dent in his personal responsibilities, despite the superimposition on the Cabinet in an earlier Administration of the National Security Council.

The Cabinet posts indicate the heads of the Departments which—huge as some may be—are the housekeeping agencies of the Government: the budget makers, training agencies, and action forces.

There is no place within them for some White House activities that are among the most critical and most expensive (except for Defense) commitments: Space, atomic development and control, the Central Intelligence Agency, among others. Plus the higher level planning between heads of governments dubbed "summit" operations.

These responsibilities centering on the White House sometimes are termed the measures of Presidential prestige. They also are an indication of the headaches and sleepless nights experienced by its occupant.

In all the ramifications of world affairs, and the nuances of domestic problems and development there is only one place where the problems eventually land—the White House.

Time and again proposals have been made to "relieve" the White House of some of the responsibilities laid upon its occupant, but they have not made much progress and probably never will—barring a complete revolution in American thought. The first reason is that the system works; the second reason is that the growing history of other forms of government seems to indicate to the essentially American conservatism that those forms are too risky.

With some slight exception for de Gaulle's changes in the French Government that may or may not outlast him, the White House is the focal point in a system literally invented by the Founding Fathers to give stability to this country.

The major democracies of countries comparable in temperament to the North American all have a parliamentary system of government. Each has a figurehead as Chief of State who signs the laws, with no right to refuse or even to argue, who gives the state banquets, makes the formal calls abroad, and delivers the speeches expressing the views of the current government. In Germany, Italy, and France, until the recent changes, this man is the President elected for a long and set term of years. In the countries of the British Commonwealth and in Holland these figureheads are the two Queens; and Kings and Queens in hereditary lines preside over lesser countries.

The President of the United States ranks equally with these foreign rulers, and in the formalities of his office he does everything they do, but it is a sideline for the White House.

The chief executives of these other countries—the political chiefs in systems as democratic in operation as that of the United States—are the Prime Ministers who while in office do all the workhorse jobs that in this country center in the White House. The central difference is in the manner of their election and some results of this that the framers of the Constitution of the United States were determined to avoid.

The other countries have a parliamentary system of government, in which voters in national elections each vote for a single individual, the member of parliament for a district. The party, or coalition of parties, that wins or forms the majority of seat holders controls the government. Voters already know the names of the party leaders among the candidates and are forewarned as to who will be the Prime Minister and his principal Secretaries.

The Prime Minister, backed by his vote control, rules until either a new election is required by expiration of time, or a parliament revolts and a new election must be called. Then everything may start all over again.

The framers of the Constitution wanted to avoid just that predicament, so they set up the President as both Chief of State and Executive—to be elected independently of votes for Congressmen and Senators. He runs for office as the head of his party. If he is lucky (and sometimes he is) the President has the majority of the votes in Congress that make him as strong a political leader as any Prime Minister. But even if he loses party control in Congress he remains in office for a set term as Chief Executive.

There have been many debates over which system is the best but, as noted heretofore, the Constitutional system has worked for a long time.

22 Women in the White House

One of the fantastic accidents of history is the role collectively played by the succession of more than thirty wives of Presidents in their successive occupancy of the White House, and the cumulative influence that they have exerted upon the American scene.

Almost all the reviews of the White House have been so concerned with the personalities, politics, and perversities of the male occupants that the roles of their wives have simply been taken for granted. If a President was married, his wife simply moved in with him, and as the home-maker she usually was given some public funds to tidy up the mansion and personalize it a little bit.

Yet, this writer feels it worthwhile to note some extraordinary developments in the unscheduled history of American women in the White House story.

Comparisons with other older governments supply few parallels. In the cases of the queens in history, almost as much care was taken to supply princes and kings with pedigreed wives as has been exercised by the breeders of horses and dogs. As of today, the result is that almost all royal mates are mutually descended from the same lists of ancestors, and share the same tastes in breeding and manners. Even in the newer European development of republics, the higher ranking officials still were elected as a rule from the privileged classes, and they brought to their posts wives from similar well-classified ranks of their national societies. In these more stratified societies there always was a definable financial as well as social background and a certain air of being-used-to the kind of life that accompanied high political position.

Some wives of American Presidents could be placed in the same category, but they can be counted in the minority. Quite a number came from financially poor backgrounds and, with the spread of the United States geographically, a number found themselves, as First Ladies, with much less knowledge of Washington than the remotest viewer of television has in his mind today.

Perhaps these heroines have been less noted in history than otherwise because, as the tabloid headline writers say, "Good girls don't make news."

A few first ladies have been noted for pretensions, in the earlier days, and a few for crude manners. But it is time to note that no mistress of the White House has been involved in any kind of marital problem, or anything as serious or sensational as a scandal involving sex. No First Lady has ever been suspected of cheating on the household accounts. None has ever figured in stories of gaucheries or bad manners affecting the affairs of the country.

The criticisms leveled at these women have been exclusively for self-involvement in the fringes of political affairs, none serious, and some occasional laughable attempts by modern standards to protect the dignity of their husbands' high office, according to the customs and manners of the times.

The impressions we have of the First Ladies of the past from the records of the eighteenth and nineteenth centuries, were more notable than often is remembered for vituperative and critical comment. Yet the worst that was written usually was of a type to arouse sympathy for these women who had to improvise at every step.

Nowhere in the Constitution is there mention of duties or limitations regarding the wife of the President. Perhaps the Founding Fathers showed some of their greatest wisdom in simply leaving this up to the women. All that existed was the general area of social precedent, and perhaps occasional long, private conversations in the late evening in whatever served as the White House family sitting room. And most First Ladies have had an uncanny knack for floating with the tides of custom.

The only First Lady never to occupy the White House was Martha Washington, and we smile when we read that the ladies who attended her levees in Philadelphia often addressed her as "Your Majesty," although there is no record that she ever asked them to do so. Yet this seems not too unusual in the atmosphere of her day and the extraordinary prestige of President Washington. The custom was dropped forever when the first Adamses succeeded the Washingtons, and Abigail —despite background and breeding that marked American "aristocracy"—made her position closely akin to that of the already traditional American housewife. Proper drying of the wash was equally as important as proper furnishing of the state parlors of the White House.

If Dolley Madison seems to have been bumptious, boisterous, and uninhibited throughout her sixteen years of White House association—as hostess first for Jefferson and subsequently with her husband—recall her era. Also, possibly her revolt against a family poverty caused by the religious conversion of her father, who left none of his estate to support his wife and daughter.

Dolley's emergence in Washington coincided with the first great boom in the wealth of the new United States, and when Europe, despite the Napoleonic Wars, was reaching its most extravagant peak of luxury. Her purchase of a coach-equivalent of a Rolls-Royce was a natural gesture that her contemporaries applauded, especially since she used it to keep the interminable round of engagements that made every other Washingtonian feel that she cared.

The reversion to formality by Elizabeth Monroe also mirrored another era, although her raised platform soon disappeared. She misgauged the American temper of the period and overshot the goal in attempting a return to elegance, but the worst criticism of her was that her British upbringing and long residence in France when her husband was Minister had given her some wrong impressions of America, or at least the America of public political life.

There is, sadly, a missing portrait among the gallery of the First Ladies. Mrs. Andrew Jackson died shortly before her husband was inaugurated. It has been noted that "she smoked a pipe," but anyone who has visited the Hermitage and

217

has seen the exquisite taste, indicating the manner of life which the Jacksons must have lived there, would want to know more about the woman whose friends bestowed on her the affectionate title of "Aunt Rachel."

Many of the Presidential wives appear from the records to have been simply negative personalities who went through the official waltz in the tight little birdcage of an ever-restricting "official life" as American manners aped more and more the cold formalities of the Victorian era. Individualities began to blossom again in the twentieth century.

It is an amazing thing that in a line of thirty-six Presidents—particularly considering the average age of these holders of public office—only one has ever suffered an illness that held him in suspenseful invalidism for a long period, Woodrow Wilson. Yet the problem of what might be done under the law to fill such a gap in the atomic age is so great that at this writing a proposed Consitutional amendment on the subject is under consideration by the States.

Mrs. Wilson is accorded general compliments for the manner in which she attempted to protect her husband, but theirs was a relatively quiet world, and Wilson went out of office with no harm having been done by his incapacity. Had there been a real crisis in the latter months of 1919 or early in 1920, the story might have been vastly different, particularly with the divisions existing between the President and the Legislative branch of the Congress. The situation resolved itself and the White House emerged a bit shaken in prestige but essentially undamaged.

There can be no argument with the statement that Mrs. Eleanor Roosevelt introduced into the history of First Ladies the prototype of the dynamic women who matured in the twentieth century. She survived long enough to become in her own right the first full-fledged diplomatic representative introduced from the ranks of Presidential widows.

Some of her friends believed that she would have gone that far even if never married to a President. Many of her critics expressed the fear that she might have gone even further in public influence if she had not been restrained by her husband's position.

Few persons remember that Eleanor Roosevelt (and that was the way she preferred to be called) had made a considerable mark as a lecturer on causes while her husband was still an invalid recuperating from his attack of infantile parilysis, suffered in 1921. In keeping with the custom of her time, as wife of a wealthy and semiprominent man, she accepted no fees. She spoke where her appearance would help gain support for youth movements, education, and women's organizations. Those who later criticized her activities and her vigor in pursuing them either were ignorant of, or chose to overlook, the long preceding years.

It was typical of her sense of humor that when a cartoon was published poking clever fun at her, it became one of her favorites. One depicted two miners underground, with one looking past his companion and exclaiming:

"Gosh! Here comes Eleanor. Now what is she doing—traveling around the world just making more trouble?"

The comments grew less than jocular when in 1935 Mrs. Roosevelt signed contracts to do a radio program and to write her newspaper column, "My Day," for pay. The fact that she arranged for the money to be paid to welfare organizations did little to still the criticism, until one of President Roosevelt's severest critics inadvertently helped to understand this woman.

Roy Howard, publisher of the Scripps-Howard newspapers, was the contractor for "My Day." He was asked why he published it, and his reply was that he felt it to be his duty to give newspaper readers both sides of controversial questions; Mrs. Roosevelt was the best interpreter of the New Deal.

But there was a depth to Mrs. Roosevelt that was not sufficiently appreciated until her widowhood. A striking incident illustrating her unplanned and spontaneous responses to the needs of others was witnessed in the White House as she was departing for Warm Springs where only a few hours earlier her husband's unexpected death had occurred.

A limousine was waiting to whisk her to an airport where a plane awaited her. In the hall of the White House a small group waited to see her off. At the forefront of this group was a shocked and perhaps frightened man filled with the responsibilities of a new office—Harry S Truman, who had been President for only a few hours.

He stepped forward and said to Mrs. Roosevelt that he and Mrs. Truman wished to do everything possible to make this period easier for her. Her reply was instantaneous: "But, Mr. President, what can we do for you?"

Aged sixty years when she was widowed, Mrs. Roosevelt soon enlarged her activities—and became anything but a quiet widow. Finally she was shaking an admonishing finger at and speaking sharp criticism to the Communist delegates to the United Nations, where she now sat as a delegate appointed by Truman. In 1952 the organizers of the Democratic National Convention designated her to give the definitive speech on the United Nations at that time, an assignment in which she humorously referred to herself as "the old lady speaking to you now." And in that speech she remarked on the cartoon showing the miners.

The setting of precedents seemed for several years to have stopped with Mrs. Roosevelt, until a new dynamism was introduced into the role of White House women by Mrs. Kennedy. Her and Mrs. Johnson's activities are too recent for reciting here.

In 1966 the role of the White House wife has expanded and been accepted as an active part of the Executive Establishment in which the occupants themselves have created the pattern. Somewhat like the common law of Great Britain, it is not written down in any statutes passed by that government, but consists of centuries of precedents and rulings which, once accepted, stand for the future.

Yet there is a creeping acceptance of the fact that in most cases where there is a President there is a woman in the White House, with official duties and responsibilities.

The first legal recognition of this situation, coming after the fact, was a law passed many years ago which gave to the widows of Presidents the right to frank their letters—to use the mail, like ranking Government officials, without payment of postage. In recent years, when Congress provided pensions for Presidents it provided also for their widows. Finally, in the light of the enormous correspondence which deluged Mrs. Kennedy after her husband's death, provision was made for an office and staff to assist her in that task.

The most recent addition to prerogatives for the widows of Presidents was provision of bodyguards to protect them from cranks or others who might harm them.

Yet all that has been done over the years has constituted in effect recognition "after the fact," as the lawyers have it.

It remains possible, just possible, that in time the woman accompanying her husband to the White House as hostess and housekeeper will be recognized by law in her own rights and responsibilities. . . . Unless, as is possible, a woman becomes President herself and opens a new chapter of the White House story for her husband in the role of unofficial "host."

In a very literal and symbolic sense, no old day ends or any new day begins in the onrushing development of the White House story.

The antennae of its communications network tingle with every new crisis, however remote geographically, and nothing that occurs anywhere on earth is remote from it. To earth, there is also being added rapidly a fair section of the relatively nearby universe, including the moon and possibly the planet Mars.

The aging mansion sometimes seems to be an anachronism in a world typified more and more by the American development of glass-and-metal skyscrapers, which even in Washington crowd close to it, although their height is still controlled. Yet it still fits peculiarly proper and right in its setting and there seems nothing strange in the multiple roles it plays as background for extraordinarily complicated and different activities.

Fortunately the external additions through the years have been made with good taste and have enhanced the dignity drawn into the original plans. In its white paint, the White House looks as new and fresh as today and, despite the fences and the guarded gates, not at all forbidding. Perhaps the semblance of newness comes from the fact that the architecture of the White House—sometimes called Federal and sometimes Greek Revival—seems to remain ever-contemporary because there is hardly an American city whose suburbs do not bristle with the porticoed miniature copies of the prototype.

The broad grounds look soft and well proportioned, with carefully spaced flower beds and the ancient elms. There is no provision for the military parades and spectacles American tourists flock abroad to see but never seem to wish for here. The only sights and sounds that seem out of place are those of helicopters. But perhaps this was said of automobiles when they displaced the coaches and carriages.

In these surroundings, officials arrive and depart with a studied unhurriedness. Informal lunches are served, and occasional formal banquets, and periodic vast receptions are held. Even the pickets who frequently parade on the sidewalk seldom speak loudly.

This is the external appearance of the new Bedlam-on-the-Potomac that is the nerve center of the free world and the inner fortress defending alike democracy abroad and the rights of the minorities in the United States.

In sum, the whole organization of the White House resembles the quiet atmosphere of an international business of long traditions, with the exception that the individual who acts as chairman of the board, as well as president and chief executive officer, lives in his own apartment within the complex. The result is that his first waking hours and his last evening ruminations, instead of being devoted to relaxation, are the busiest hours of report reading, reflection, and resolution.

At the moment in history when this book was being completed, toward the close of 1965, the White House stood at the center of a host of "crises" requiring some daily attention. Each was a test of delicate consideration ranging from international diplomacy to crucial decisions being forced or encouraged in domestic affairs.

None was remote from the White House, however, because of the accretion of power and authority that had brought it to its ever-heightening peak of authority and prestige.

Asia threatened to become the chronic crisis of a world in which American commitments often had been undertaken reluctantly but nevertheless could not be diminished or abandoned. And the Asian commitments seemed often to run in contradictory lines to each other.

Across that continent were deployed the contending forces of Russia, China, India, Pakistan, and the United States. In Vietnam the United States was engaged in what had become a full-scale war, assisting that small country to defend itself against a Communist twin in North Vietnam which had invaded its territory with guerillas, and fought with heavy support alike from China and Russia. Diplomatically, Russia stood in general stance as a friend of the United States in the affairs of the Western World but as strong and vocal ally of China in supporting North Vietnam, although deeply divided from the Chinese Communist regime on other matters.

India and Pakistan, both largely restored economically and armed by the United States for presumed defense against China, had clashed in war in mid-1965, but agreed to a tenuous cease-fire. In this conflict, China had intervened by a foray against India, which brought the strongest verbal protests from Russia.

To the eastward in Asia, Borneo was challenging the American-British Commonwealth alliance attempting to maintain the independence of Malaysia and Singapore, at a time when the hard-pressed British Government was proclaiming its absolute need to cut down military commitments "east of Suez." Yet Britain and Canada were working closely on a friendly basis with Communist China. Japan, almost an economic creation of the United States's restorative work after World War II, was working closely in strong cooperation and increasing trade with China and opposing bitterly the South Vietnam commitment.

In Western Europe there were the daily crises of negotition over monetary problems, the question of survival of great recent plans for economic cooperation within Europe, and everlasting debates over control, on the one hand, by treaty on atomic weapons, and demands, on the other, for ever wider development of these under additional flags.

Latin American affairs flowed through the White House as efforts were made to patch up Pan American relations on one side with the replacement of a treaty over the Panama Canal that always had irked that little country, but each step of progress seemed to be hurt by other developments, such as efforts to gain unity on opposition to Communism by policies to apply force against other prospective Cuban coups. The Dominican Republic, after a bloody revolution, still writhed in efforts to achieve stable government.

At home in its own frontyard, the White House also faced conflicts, in the manner of handling the massive antipoverty program, the making of civil rights fully and universally effective, the complete integration of schools and public and private service, and the great effort to end more hidden but equally serious discrimination. . . . Plus such matters—affecting relatively small groups but still big issues—as granting the rights of citizenship in political affairs to the District of Columbia.

The matters just outlined each held at times such explosive possibilities that daily attention at the top was absolutely essential. Whether the need was to translate programs into more legislation, to send greater numbers of troops, airplanes, and weapons into world troublespots, to cajole or force contending friends into amicable relationships if not friendship—each required study, discussion, and decision. It was more than any one man could do, and accordingly the White House was becoming more and more the prisoner of its advisers and sometimes the symbol of contention among them. All this constitutes what we mean by the term "the White House."

Soon after his succession to the Presidency, Harry Truman sat one day in an off-the-record press conference—genuinely off the record. It was a seminar to help reporters make some sense out of an annual budget already printed and ready for presentation to the Congress. Truman prefaced the explanations by the experts flanking him with some comments on the Presidency. The writer was present. No notes were made of these remarks, but recollection makes a clear paraphrase possible:

This Budget [Truman commented] is a document in fine print considerably thicker than the largest city telephone directory. It includes every nickel the Government proposes to spend in the next fiscal year right down to the last messenger's salary. It is the President's Budget, and the President is supposed to account for all its details to the Congress.

But what does the President know about its contents? He knows what all the Departments and Bureaus have reported that they need or wish, and have fought out to some degree with the Bureau of the Budget. And who made up the contents? The chiefs and assistant chiefs and the technical specialists.

Do you know how many such officials there are in the Government—the men who report to the President either directly or through their superiors, but who carry some individual executive or administrative responsibility in the name of the President?

It is important to remember the number because you would think that each such officer should be reasonably close to the President, either to give advice when asked for it or to seek advice from the President.

Well, the number is about *four thousand*. That means [Truman concluded] that if I averaged an hour each in conferences with these officials, it would take two years of average working days to see them one at a time.

The practical result of this problem, in later times when bureaucracy has grown   *223* much larger, is that White House decisions are based on a changing but relatively narrow group of close-in advisers, and that some relatively important officials may go for years with no more than a friendly nod from the President at a large gathering. Even the rank and designation of Cabinet members sometimes becomes relatively meaningless, or the emphasis in importance shifts with personalities and problems.

For generations, up to World War II, the White House was the center of a fairly tidy operation served by a small Cabinet, whose members could keep relatively close tabs on the Departments and be prepared to keep the President reasonably well informed, especially on those matters with which he must deal with Congress, such as appropriations, foreign policy, and the domestic economy.

The flurry of expansion in 1917–18 made a need for more space for administrative help in the military, but even that war hardly disturbed the sense of intimacy in the official family.

The Secretary of State was the most prestigious member of that family, followed more or less in importance by the Secretaries of War and Navy, the Secretary of the Treasury, the Postmaster General, and the Attorney General. Around the turn of the century, when Congress established the primary regulatory agencies over transportation, foods and drugs, and interestate commerce, it set up "independent agencies" directly accountable to itself.

Later on Commerce and Agriculture were made the responsibilities of Departments, and most recently Health, Education, and Welfare were combined as one, plus Urban Affairs. In the meantime, the old Departments of War and Navy were combined for convenience of Presidential liaison in the Department of Defense, which took in the Army and the Navy as Subdivisions and added a third equal subdivision for Air.

Still the Cabinet remained relatively small, and more streamlining was done by combining all the now numerous former "independent agencies" under the White House wing, which accounts for the great space required in the Executive Office Building.

Yet the White House responsibilities continue to get out of hand, and depend more and more on the personalities of the men selected by the President to fill both the traditional and the formerly unknown responsibilities of the White House.

There is the Central Intelligence Agency whose highly secret but vast field and personnel include both gathering of vital information for the Government and the direction of many policy actions. Atomic energy and Space each spend money and conduct operations as great or greater than some Departments.

Agriculture, HEW, and Urban all have become great spending and control operations in an era when the Federal Government penetrates virtually every phase of American life. The Justice Department, which was formed for the two simple purposes of prosecuting federal crime and defending before the Supreme Court challenges of constitutionality of laws, now dips even to the county level in civil rights activities, and shelters in one branch the Federal Bureau of Investigation.

And all of these technically are the

Executive responsibilities of the abstraction officially known as the White House.

To coordinate the overlapping work of this conglomeration, the White House established a sort of inner Cabinet known as the National Security Council, and also set up a corps of assistants in the White House offices who rank above the official White House secretaries but below —sometimes only slightly below—the members of the Cabinet.

How much this streamlining can accomplish has never been determined. The only forseeable outlook is one in which the President must act as a day-to-day figurative fireman devoting most of his time to the major crises that come to his desk and trusting to assistants to see that all goes relatively well in routine matters.

There is a tradition surrounding the White House that its occupant, as the sole Federal official elected directly by the American public, is a leader in policy direction and the Chief Executive in carrying out the laws passed by Congress. His Messages to Congress, delivered annually on the State of the Nation and with the Budget, formerly constituted highly important and almost sacred statements on the problems and needs of the times. They have come in more recent years to present progress reports, often supplemented or amended by dozens of other intermediate Messages.

The importance of the White House in leadership depends very largely on the cooperation with, or control over, Congress exercised from year to year by the President. However, time and circumstances—what we now recognize as a world-wide demand for change and betterment—have thrust the White House into a new role as a crusader. And this has become probably the most demanding role thrust on the President. There is no longer much argument as to the propriety of the newer role of leadership, and neither is it so very new; it simply grows more pronounced.

It was not Kennedy or F. D. Roosevelt or Teddy Roosevelt alone who started the trends for broader interpretation of civil rights and economic protection for individuals, for "busting the trusts" or regulating interstate commerce or hunting ways to protect agricultural prices or enforcing the payment of minimum wages, or providing various types of care for the aged and the helpless in American society.

These are programs that grew out of generations of debate and demand, often urged far ahead of Presidential programs on the floors of the Senate and House, or springing out of demands by the States.

In most of these cases, the White House has reacted rather than initiated. The Presidents who have been most noted for leadership in progressive reforms have in many cases been the most skilled political interpreters of the winds of change in public thought.

In the period covered by this summary of the White House story, every major country in the world has undergone revolutionary reforms and changes and— with the exception of Great Britain—vast political changes usually involving armed revolution.

Perhaps the greatest aspect of the whole White House story has been its symbolism of a national state of mind that has been able to weather political change in peace.   225

This compilation starts with George Washington, although his terms expired before the White House became the residence of the President of the United States.

The information includes the pertinent dates of birth, period in office, and death, as well as related statistics, where known, of the wives of the Presidents. Also, the size of their families.

1. GEORGE WASHINGTON. 1789–1797. Born February 22, 1732, at Wakefield, Westmoreland County, Virginia. He married the widow Martha Dandridge Custis, a wealthy woman his own age, in 1759. They had no children of their own. Martha had lost two children in infancy, but when she married Washington she had a daughter, Martha, and a son, John Parke Custis. Her daughter died when seventeen and her son died in 1781 from wounds received in the battle of Yorktown. Washington adopted John's son, whose daughter would marry Robert E. Lee. Washington died in 1799.

2. JOHN ADAMS. 1797–1801. Born October 30, 1735, in Braintree, Massachusetts. He married Abigail Smith, of Weymouth, Massachusetts. They had three sons and two daughters. One son, J. Q. Adams, became the sixth President of the United States. John Adams died in 1826.

3. THOMAS JEFFERSON. 1801–1809. Born April 13, 1743, at Shadwell, Virginia. He married in 1772 a twenty-three-year-old widow, Mrs. Martha Wales.

They had six children but only two lived to maturity. Jefferson died on the same day and in the same year as John Adams, July 4, 1836.

4. JAMES MADISON. 1809–1817. Born March 16, 1751, at Port Conway, King George County, Virginia, the eldest of twelve children. He married the widowed Dolley Payne Todd in 1794 at Philadelphia. They had no children. Madison died on June 28, 1836, but Dolley survived him until 1849.

5. JAMES MONROE. 1817–1825. Born April 28, 1758, in Westmoreland County, Virginia. He was the first combat veteran of the Revolution to become President, having been wounded at Trenton fighting with the Third Virginia Regiment. He studied law under Thomas Jefferson. In 1786 he married Elizabeth Kortwright, of New York. Their family consisted of two daughters. Monroe died in 1831, the third President to pass away on July 4, one year after the death of his wife.

6. JOHN QUINCY ADAMS. 1825–1829. Born in the house of his father, John Adams, at Braintree, Massachusetts, July 11, 1767. He married in 1797, the twenty-two-year-old Louisa Catherine Johnson, of Maryland. He died February 23, 1848, leaving three sons and one daughter. His widow survived until 1852.

7. ANDREW JACKSON. 1829–1837. Born in North Carolina, March 15, 1767, he finally made his home in Tennessee, at the estate known as the Hermitage, which he began developing with the building of

a log cabin. Jackson married in 1791 Mrs. Lewis Robards, the separated wife of Colonel Lewis Robards and daughter of Colonel John Donelson, of Nashville, Tennessee. A misunderstanding about the Robards' divorce led Jackson and Rachel to remarry in 1793. Jackson had no children, but adopted his sister's son. Mrs. Jackson died between her husband's election and his Inaugural. Jackson lived until June 8, 1845.

8. MARTIN VAN BUREN. 1837–1841. Born on December 5, 1782, at Kinderhook, New York. He married in 1807 Hannah Hoes, of New York, who bore him four sons before she died in 1819. Van Buren lived until July 24, 1862.

9. WILLIAM HENRY HARRISON. Served only thirty-one days in 1841 before dying. Born February 9, 1773, in Berkeley, Charles City County, Virginia. In 1795 he married Anna Symmes, a native of New Jersey. The Harrisons had six sons and four daughters. Mrs. Harrison never lived in the White House. She had planned to delay going to Washington until after her husband's Inaugural. She survived him by twenty-three years, until 1864.

10. JOHN TYLER. 1841–1845. Born March 29, 1790, in Greenway, Charles City County, Virginia. Tyler married first Letitia Christian, by whom he had three sons and four daughters, in addition to two children who died in infancy. They were married in 1813. Mrs. Tyler died in 1842 in the White House. In 1844 Tyler married Julia Gardiner, then twenty-four years of age, who bore five sons and two daughters. Tyler died January 18, 1862.

11. JAMES KNOX POLK. 1845–1849. Born November 2, 1795, in Mecklenburg County, North Carolina. He married in 1824 Sarah Childress, who prohibited dancing or the serving of liquor in the White House. They had no children. He died June 15, 1849.

12. ZACHARY TAYLOR. Born in Orange County, Virginia, on November 24, 1784, he lived for only sixteen months of his Presidency, dying of typhus July 9, 1850. He married in 1810 Margaret Smith, the daughter of a Maryland planter. They had a family of one son and five daughters.

13. MILLARD FILLMORE. 1850–1853. Born January 7, 1800, in a log cabin on a farm in Cayuga County, New York. After his father had apprenticed him to a dyer, he finally bought his freedom for thirty dollars and became a teacher. Fillmore's first wife was Abigail Powers, of New York, who bore one son and one daughter, and who died in 1853. His second wife, a widow whom he married in 1858, was Mrs. Caroline Carmichael McIntosh. He died on March 8, 1874.

14. FRANKLIN PIERCE. 1853–1857. Born in Hillsboro, New Hampshire, on November 23, 1804. He married in 1834 Miss Jane Means Appleton, of New Hampshire, daughter of the President of Bowdoin College. They had three sons but one died in infancy, one at the age of four, and the third was killed in a railroad accident at eleven. Pierce died October 8, 1869.

15. JAMES BUCHANAN. 1857–1861. Born near Mercersburg, Pennsylvania, on April 23, 1791. A lifelong bachelor, he died on June 1, 1868.

16. ABRAHAM LINCOLN. 1861–April 15, 1865. Born on a farm in Hardin County, Kentucky, February 12, 1809. He was married November 4, 1842, to Mary Todd. They had four sons. Lincoln was assassinated in the second month of his second term.

17. ANDREW JOHNSON. 1865–1869. Born in Raleigh, North Carolina, December 29, 1808. He was married in 1827 to Eliza McCardle, and they had three sons and two daughters. He died on July 31, 1875.

18. ULYSSES S. GRANT. 1869–1877. Born at Point Pleasant, Ohio, on April 27, 1822. He married Julia Dent, of St. Louis, Missouri, in 1848. They had three sons and one daughter. He died on July 23, 1885.

19. RUTHERFORD BIRCHARD HAYES. 1877–1881. Born at Delaware, Ohio, on October 4, 1822. He married Lucy Webb, of Chillicothe, Ohio, in 1852. They had seven sons and one daughter. He died on January 17, 1893.

20. JAMES ABRAM GARFIELD. March 4, 1881–September 19, 1881. Garfield, the second President to be assassinated, was born in Orange, Cuyahoga County, Ohio, on November 19, 1831. Garfield was married to Lucretia Rudolph, of Ohio, in 1858. They had four sons and one daughter.

21. CHESTER ALAN ARTHUR. 1881–1885. Born at Fairfield, Vermont, on October 5, 1830. He was married in 1859 to Ellin Lewis Herndon, who died in 1880. They had two sons and one daughter. Arthur died November 18, 1886.

22. GROVER CLEVELAND. 1885–1889. Born at Caldwell, New Jersey, March 18, 1837. Cleveland is the only President to have served two terms that were not consecutive. By official ruling, he is both the twenty-second and the twenty-fourth Presidents. He was a bachelor when he began his first term. He was married to Frances Folsom on June 2, 1886. They had two sons and three daughters. Cleveland died on June 24, 1908, but Mrs. Cleveland lived until 1947.

23. BENJAMIN HARRISON. 1889–1893. Born at North Bend, Ohio, on August 20, 1833. Harrison was married twice: first to Caroline Lavinia Scott, of Ohio, in 1853. She died in the White House in 1892. Their family consisted of one son and one daughter. Harrison subsequently married his wife's niece, Mrs. Mary Scott Lord Dimmock, of New York, whose first husband had died in 1882, and who bore Harrison a daughter. Harrison died on March 13, 1901.

24. GROVER CLEVELAND. 1893–1897.

25. WILLIAM McKINLEY. 1897–September 14, 1901. The third President to be assassinated—after little more than six months in his second term—was born at Niles, Ohio, on January 29, 1843. He was married to Ida Saxton, of Ohio, in 1871. They had two daughters.

26. THEODORE ROOSEVELT. 1901–1909. Roosevelt was born in New York City on October 27, 1858. His first wife, whom he married in 1881 and who died in 1884, was the mother of Alice Roosevelt Longworth. In 1886 he married Edith Kermit Carow, who bore him four sons. Theodore Roosevelt died January 6, 1919.

27. WILLIAM HOWARD TAFT. 1909–1913. Born at Cincinnati, Ohio, on September 15, 1857. He was married

in 1886 to Helen Herron, a musician and later a founder of the Cincinnati orchestra. The Tafts had two sons and one daughter—one son being Senator Robert A. Taft. W. H. Taft died March 8, 1930, after post-Presidential service as Associate Justice of the Supreme Court.

28. WOODROW WILSON. 1913–1921. Born at Staunton, Virginia, December 28, 1856, but later settled in New Jersey. Wilson married in 1885 Ellen Louise Axson, of Virginia. They had three daughters. The first Mrs. Wilson died in the White House in 1914. In 1915 Wilson married Edith Bolling Galt. He died on February 3, 1924.

29. WARREN GAMALIEL HARDING. 1921–August 2, 1923. Harding was born near Blooming Grove (later Corsica), Ohio, on November 2, 1865. He married Mrs. Florence Kling De Wolfe, at Marion, Ohio, in 1891. They had no children. Harding died in San Francisco as a result of illness that had forced him to halt for rest after returning from a trip to Alaska.

30. CALVIN COOLIDGE. 1923–1929. Coolidge was born at Plymouth, Vermont, July 4, 1872. He married, in 1905, Grace Anna Goodhue. They had two sons, one of whom died of an infection in the White House. Coolidge died on January 5, 1933.

31. HERBERT CLARK HOOVER. 1929–1933. Hoover was born at West Branch, Iowa, on August 10, 1874. He married in 1899 Lou Henry, also an Iowa native. They had two sons. Hoover died in 1965, surviving his wife by twenty-one years.

32. FRANKLIN DELANO ROOSEVELT. 1933–April 12, 1945. The only President to be elected to a fourth term, F. D. Roosevelt was born near Hyde Park, New York, January 30, 1882. He married Eleanor Roosevelt, a remote cousin and niece of Theodore Roosevelt, in 1905. They had four sons and one daughter. Roosevelt died at his cottage at Warm Springs unexpectedly and while resting in preparation for the San Francisco meeting to form the United Nations.

33. HARRY S TRUMAN. 1945–1953. Truman was born at Lamar, Missouri, on May 8, 1884. He was married to Bess Wallace, of Missouri, in 1919. They are both living as of this writing (1966) and have one daughter, Margaret, Mrs. Clifton Daniel.

34. DWIGHT DAVID EISENHOWER. 1953–1961. Born at Denison, Texas, on October 14, 1890. In 1916 he married Mamie Geneva Doud. They have one son. At this writing they live on a farm near Gettysburg, Pennsylvania.

35. JOHN FITZGERALD KENNEDY. 1961–November 22, 1963. The fourth President to be assassinated was born in Brookline, Massachusetts, on May 29, 1917. He married in 1953 Jacqueline Bouvier, of New York. They had two children, a daughter, Caroline, and a son, John F., Jr., who was born in November 1960, between the dates of his father's election and his inauguration. Kennedy was murdered by a sniper, while on a visit to Dallas, Texas.

36. LYNDON B. JOHNSON. 1963–

This President won office in his own right in the election of 1964, after serving out Kennedy's unexpired term. He was born August 27, 1908, near Stonewall, Texas. He was married in 1934 to Claudia Taylor, of Texas. They have two daughters, Lynda Bird and Luci Baines Johnson.

Picture Sources

Index

232

234

239

DATE DUE	